The *Géographe* and
the *Naturaliste* sailing
in heavy seas
with furled sails.
Drawing by Charles
Alexandre Lesueur,
illustrator with the
Baudin expedition that
sailed around Australia
(1800-1804).

Unknown Lands

The Log Books of the Great Explorers

FRANÇOIS BELLEC

Translated by Lisa Davidson and Elizabeth Ayre

The Overlook Press
WOODSTOCK & NEW YORK

Contents

7   Introduction

12   The Book of the East Indies

56   The Book of the New World

102   The Book of Disillusionment

140   The Book of Misconceptions

182   Scientific Expeditions

214   Photographic credits and illustrations

Dutch ship from
the second half of
the sixteenth century.
Engraving by
Frans Huys, circa 1564,
after Pieter Bruegel

This book is not a historical overview of the discoveries and exploration of the world, although each chapter covers major events in the gradual investigation of the mythical space that had, since Antiquity, been known as the "Sea of Darkness." Maritime expansion, on which European nations have based their collective culture and national heritage, can be credited to both ordinary and extraordinary men, who had no inkling as to the scale of the hitherto unknown world. Most are anonymous, while the names of a few heroes have been stamped indelibly into the annals of history. They were called *conquistadores, descobridores,* or merely adventurers, and later, explorers.

Their logs and correspondence, along with stories by their companions, radiate with the spontaneity of sincere emotion and wonder, along with the superlatives that these new worlds inspired. We read of their noble motivations, occasional arrogant pride, confidence, doubts, weariness, fears, confusion, failures, and at times distress. These writings, spanning five centuries, were the first accounts of the vast unknown land that challenged the understanding of European culture.

This book does not aim to analyze the long-term consequences of these discoveries on Europe's expansion, but lingers instead on the discoverers themselves. It is based on their own stories, to capture as authentically as possible what they actually felt as they wrote, before their successes or failures had had any perceptible impact on the larger world. The discoverers recorded their log entries before knowing that Hispaniola would become the Americas; before realizing that an immense ocean stretched across the other side of the continent; before the myth of the *Terra Australis Incognita* was debunked; before the disappearance of the Lapérouse expedition, lost to an unknown reef; and before the "discovery" of the tobacco plant, described rather absent-mindedly by the explorers. I greatly respect these men; theirs was an infinitely humbling experience.

The events we call "the discoveries" took place over a period that spanned slightly less than two centuries. It began in the late Middle Ages, as the Renaissance spread north from the Mediterranean, laying the foundations for a new European culture. Through the early years of the sixteenth century, all expeditions set sail from the Iberian peninsula, starting in 1415 from Ceuta on the Moroccan shores of the Strait of Gibraltar. This region had just been captured by Portuguese troops led by the Infante Henry, who would later be known as "Henry the Navigator." One century later, these discoverers had reached Canton, the ultimate goal of a long series of maritime operations. The motivations of this state-supported campaign were inspired by the desire for the wealth of the Far East and the religious zeal of the Crusades.

After one hundred years of intense efforts, Portugal discovered a passage from the Atlantic Ocean to the East, dispelling numerous myths in the process. During this period, more precise maps were created, new navigational techniques developed, as well as new ships. Sagres, in southern Portugal, became the hub of the "Age of Discovery."

Christopher Columbus wanted to offer an alternative to Portugal's successful circumnavigation of Africa. The idea was first proposed in 1474 by the Italian navigator Toscanelli, who thought it possible to reach China by sailing westward. The court of King John II of Portugal was the only one that could entertain this idea, as the Portuguese were the only sailors at the time who mastered the high seas. Columbus had learned this new art of sailing and its basic techniques in Lisbon. Yet Portugal had been pursuing this sea route for far too long to accept Columbus's services and to undertake a simultaneous exploration of a second passage. Furthermore, the country did not have the financial resources for such a costly undertaking: at the time, Portugal was a small country with slightly over one million inhabitants.

Thus the second wave of exploration was, rather accidentally, Spanish. It continued through the early seventeenth century when Pedro Fernandez de Queiros proposed the last in the line of idealistic projects of discovery, before the more mercantile era of the Indies trading companies. His estimable yet marginal proposal in 1606 was to found a Christian colony on the *Terra Australis Incognita*, long believed to be an undiscovered continent in the region around what is now Australia, a myth inherited from Greek geographers.

Henry the Navigator was a contemporary of Van Eyck and Donatello. Magellan was three years older than Raphael; they both died young, within one year of each other. Christopher Columbus and Leonardo da Vinci were only a few months apart in age, like Erasmus, Machiavelli, and Vasco da Gama, all born in 1469. While the frontiers of the known world were expanding, Michelangelo, Raphael, and Titian were painting the masterpieces of our civilization. Pico della Mirandola, Erasmus, and Thomas More were creating the foundations for an entirely new system of philosophy. In Florence, Cosimo, Piero, and Lorenzo de' Medici had founded a family dynasty that embodied the spirit of the Renaissance. These brilliant men, busy constructing what would become the landmarks of European culture, exchanged ideas and shared their enthusiasms. The new artistic and philosophical concepts that had shaken the old Europe, along with the technical innovations and psychological triumphs that had pushed back the frontiers of the oceans, were in perfect creative harmony. Yet they co-existed at best. The ships of the discoverers were not carried by the

An anonymous cartographer drew this map circa 1590; it is crowned by a fool's cap and illuminated by a concise biblical excerpt: *Stultorum infinitus est numerus.* If there were countless crazy men, the New World could have remained nothing more than a vast utopia.

winds of the humanists, and the latter were only remotely interested in the events that carried uneducated sailors and unscrupulous adventurers to lands inhabited by illiterate indigenous populations. The Renaissance referred to ancient Athens with delight. Spanish *conquistadores*, Portuguese *descobridores*, and humanists were supremely indifferent to one another. Florence, therefore, cannot take credit for discovering the Americas.

The discovery of new lands, including the Spanish-owned Americas, was a consequence of the somewhat earlier Portuguese overseas expansion. It was a long road beset with myths and hypotheses, along with material, scientific, and health problems, which were beyond the knowledge of Mediterranean civilization. It began when Portugal started to explore the Atlantic; the first step began in 1415 and ended in 1488 with the discovery of the Cape of Good Hope. These seventy-three years were marked by unbelievable technical and intellectual progress that could not be measured in years, but in generations.

The Portuguese exploits puts into perspective Christopher Columbus's ocean crossing—which was, nonetheless, a great feat of exploration and a tremendous gift to the sovereigns under whose flag he sailed. The Genoese navigator had almost everything wrong concerning the parameters of his project.

In the seventeenth century, the economic and political supremacy of the conquering Mediterranean Catholic countries was starting to tilt toward the younger, more liberal and mercantile-minded Protestant countries along the North Sea. Propelled by the spectacular rise of the Dutch, particularly the city of Amsterdam, merchants throughout the century relied on the discoveries made in the earlier era. Except for continuing navigational challenges, there were few new surprises. While its merchants continued trading, the Dutch East India Company continued investigating the hypothetical *Terra Australis Incognita*.

The systematic exploration of the Pacific Ocean beginning in the first two decades of the eighteenth century became a great scientific quest, fueled by the encyclopedic spirit of the time. France and England maintained a constant presence in the South Pacific through the nineteenth century, each one contributing to the progress in navigational techniques.

Thousands of sailors perished in the quest to discover new worlds, drowned if they were lucky, or parched to death by drought, gutted by dysentery, consumed by fever, martyred on uncharted lands, or ravaged by scurvy. "In Goa," reported François Pyrard de Laval in 1715, "I saw ships reach port; of the one thousand or twelve hundred men who had boarded the ship at Lisbon, no more than two hundred remained—and these men were almost all suffering from scurvy, which had so undermined their health that few even survived after they arrived."

Ship logs are generally mute about the suffering. Yet modest and sometimes eloquent glimpses of emotions, doubts and certainties, knowledge and errors, and unimaginable discoveries are offered. An unknown land rises into view on the horizon, finally opening the passage long-sought to the Indies; or under a new sky, friendly natives, exotic birds, fruit, and an infinite number of strange things appear on a white beach, proof that the sailors had not seen a mirage. They may have wept with gratitude during these rare moments, justifying the years of planning, trials, intrigues, ridicule, and endless work—not to mention days, weeks, or months at sea in conditions of extreme discomfort and doubt. The austerity of these ocean voyages, amid the noxious odor of decks overloaded with putrid food, made the view of land and the scent of lush vegetation almost unbelievably paradisiacal.

Simply to reach one's destination was a major accomplishment for the missionaries who set out to conquer souls in the New World and the scientists who later catalogued the multitude of new specimens and information collected. Captains of these high-risk ventures were obsessed with bringing their ships, crews, harvest of scientific data, or precious cargo safely into port, often noticeable between the confidently written lines in their logs. Perhaps it is hard to understand why so many sailors, working as ordinary crewmen, voluntarily signed on for these terrible torments; but from the docks of Lisbon to Portsmouth, Amsterdam, and Lorient, the discovery and exploration of exotic lands must have been tempting, to say the least.

Treasures of the Sea, an allegorical painting by Jacopo Zucchi (1541-1590). This allegory is one of the few works dealing with the exoticism and wealth of the new worlds; most Renaissance artists were only mildly interested in this subject.

Preceding double page:
*Detail of Saint Ursula
the Martyr and the Eleven
Thousand Virgins.* Santa
Auta altarpiece, from the
chapel in Lisbon's Madre
de Deus monastery.

Left:
This painting
on parchment is by
Francesco di Antionio
del Cherico, for the Latin
translation of Ptolemy's
Cosmographia by
Jacopo d'Angelo around
1465-1470. It reveals
the significant missing
geographical and
intellectual information
that would be provided
by the Renaissance
discoverers, as the
Portuguese reached the
Gulf of Guinea.

Right:
One of the rare portraits of
D. Joào II,
who played a decisive role
in the adventure of
the Portuguese discoverers.
During his reign, Elmina
fortress (in present-day
Ghana) was constructed
(1481-1495), and
Bartholomeu Dias rounded
the Cape of Good Hope.
Illuminated manuscript
from the *Livro dos Copos,*
fifteenth century (after
1485).

The discovery of the New World has, since the late fifteenth century, overshadowed the incomparable human exploit represented by the discovery of the sea route to the East Indies. The Portuguese contribution was not the discovery of an unknown continent, but rather, the invention of the navigational techniques necessary to master the sea and to find a way to reach the Indies via a direct ocean route. Paradoxically, Portuguese fame rested on such intangible events as crossing the invisible barrier formed by the "Sea of Darkness" and the fleeting wakes left behind as the ships glided over the vast empty ocean. These impalpable and silent events immortalized the navigators; they led the way to European expansion around the world. Their first great discovery was the ocean, making ocean-going voyages common.

For many years preceding the Portuguese discovery, European markets were only indirectly linked to the silk and spice routes. The route across the steppes skirted the Caspian Sea to the north, reaching the Black Sea at the mouth of the Don River or at nearby Trabizon, both of which were part of Byzantium. North of Tibet, the desert route bypassed the desolate expanse of the Takla Makan, crossed the Pamir, went through Tashkent and Samarkand, and finally, in northern Afghanistan, joined up with the southern route that came up from the Ganges and Indus valleys. The final relay, via Baghdad, arrived at the eastern Mediterranean via Palmyra. A little-known sea route stretched from China to Arabia, traveled by an inextricable network of Chinese, Indian, Persian, and Arab vessels. Cargo was unloaded from ships in the Red Sea and Persian Gulf and transferred to caravans heading to Alexandria, Beirut, or Antioch.

Trade had been controlled by Venetian merchants since the thirteenth century when, in 1204, Byzantium was conquered with help from the fourth wave of crusaders. Venice had also effectively eliminated Genoa from the commerce and held a monopoly on trade with the East. The Venetian galleys traveled to the eastern Mediterranean to pick up goods from the caravans and sold them as far away as Flanders. For Westerners, the sea extended no farther than the coastline outside the Mediterranean Sea toward northern Europe, while the Atlantic Ocean disappeared somewhere beyond the limits of the inhabitable world as defined by the Greeks.

Portugal was a small country for such a large destiny. To have rounded Cape Bojador nineteen years after capturing Ceuta, circumnavigate Africa, claim the land for Portugal, and thereby reach the Indies through the back door required a strong will and adventurous spirit. Under the successive reigns of Alfonso V and John II, the Portuguese caravels, bearing on their sails the cross of the Order of Christ, reached the equator in 1471, fifty-six years and two generations after the start of the adventure. By crossing this legendary line into the southern hemisphere, they traveled for the first time on the hidden side of the earth. Vasco da Gama reached Calicut in 1498, the final leg of the circumnavigation of Africa that had required successive expeditions spanning a period of eighty-three years and four generations. It took the Portuguese ninety-seven years to reach the Spice Islands (Moluccas), where they found cloves and nutmeg; one hundred and one years to reach "Cathay," or northern China; and twenty-six more before setting foot on Japan—the "Cipango" with golden palaces, as described by Marco Polo.

While it is generally thought that Vasco da Gama discovered the East Indies for Henry the Navigator, just as Christopher Columbus claimed the Americas for Isabella of Castile and Ferdinand of Aragon, the Indies had been "discovered" centuries earlier by Alexander the Great; the Infante Henry had been dead nearly forty years when Vasco da Gama's fleet anchored off Calicut.

ROUNDING CAPE BOJADOR

No journal entries survive to tell us how Gil Eanes of Lagos, a squire from Henry the Navigator's household, and a handful of fellow sailors, felt the day they rounded Cape Bojador in 1434. Before them, at least fifteen other ships had tried passing this cape, only to return home. They merely had to dare to go beyond the accepted boundary of Mediterranean navigation. According to old superstitions, beyond this point the sun would turn the skin of men black and a powerful current would pull ships toward the equator where the sea and air boiled as if in an immense cauldron. The end of the world lay along the latitude of Morocco and the Canary Islands.

Like the first jet pilot to break the sound barrier, the Portuguese had no idea what they would face on the other side—although they expected the worst. Eanes made two attempts before succeeding. "Although the feat was a small one in itself, it must be reckoned as great on account of its daring," the chronicler Zurara would later report. The squire hurried back to report his success to Henry. "And I told him in detail how the voyage took place and how, once we put the longboat in the water, we landed on shore, where we found no signs of habitation or people. And because, my Lord," continued Gil Eanes, "it seemed to me that I should return with some evidence from this land, because I had set

The hemisphere granted to the king of Portugal according to the clauses of the Treaty of Tordesillas (1492). The amillary sphere, represented several times on this illuminated manuscript, symbolized the opening of the world by the Portuguese. It was given to the duke of Beja, the future Manuel I, by D. Joào II, as a sign of continuity in the conquest of the route to the Indies.
Miniature of the *Chronica del Rei D. Afonso Henriques* by Duarte Galvào. First quarter of the sixteenth century.

ITEM
TROME
ALES

Proleguo dereçido ao sere
nissimo e muito poderoso
principe elRey dom manuell nosso senhor de vida e excellente ...
de portuguall ...
e espritos per ... mandado per duarte gal-
uam fidallguo de sua casa de ...
No quall falla ...
Materea que he o propio e verdadeiro louuor
de sy mesmo — Reis de portuguall

muito quem serenissimo Senhor trabalhar os
homens por em sua vida obrarem uertudes
que mereçam ade no outro mundo E neste
uiuem de seu tempo Memoria nam ...
que as alimarias tem per ... com nosso Mas que bem
e louuadamente uiueram que he propio do homem o quall
tempo a vida e no dias breue com auertude ... faz longua
durar mais de que ... viuemos depois de morto No outro
mundo per gloria e neste per exemplo ... que pera nos necessa
rio nos he ... uirtuosa
fama ... isto como ... que a todos conuem Muito mais cabe
aos principes e Reis ... fazello cuja maior excelencia de ...
Nome diz ... maior ... de seu catiuo que he ...
Reys postos per ... Reynos e principados ...
os outros homens pera exercam e exemplo de uertude Mas ...

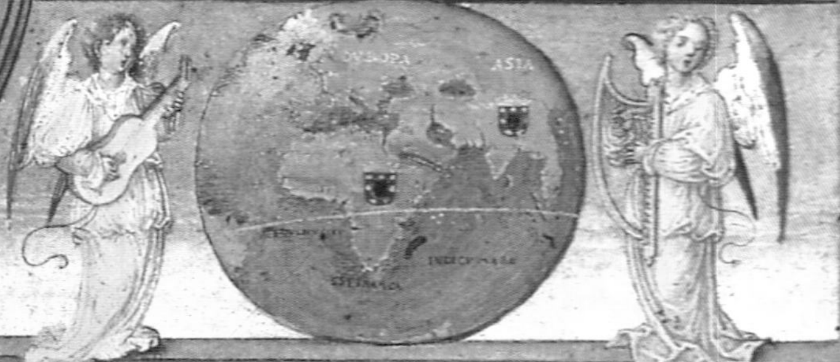

Nevertheless, although embarked
aboard ship—and these were
men who had earned reputations
for their feats as soldiers—
not one dared go beyond this cape.
And the truth be told, it was
not for lack of courage or
determination, but because it was
something completely new and
complicated by ancient legends that
had been circulating among
Spanish sailors for generations.
Although these legends were false,
the idea of verifying them seemed
fraught with danger; they wondered
who would be the first to want
to gamble his life on such an
adventure… "What benefit could
the loss of our bodies and
our souls be to the Infante?" they
asked, "as we would clearly have been
comitting suicide."

Gomes Eanes de Zurara (known as Azurara),
Crónica da Guiné (Chronicle of the Discovery of Guinea)
circa 1453.

Preceding page:
Aboard the *Boa Esperança*,
a replica of a fifteenth-
century Portuguese
discovery ship, the caravel.
The crosses painted on
the sails are those of the
Order of Christ, which
was governed by
Henry the Navigator.

Left:
A Portuguese argosy or *nau*
at anchor.
Preceding double page:
Detail of *Saint Ursula the
Martyr and the Eleven
Thousand Virgins*. Santa
Auta altarpiece, from the
chapel in Lisbon's Madre
de Deus monastery,
attributed to Cristovào de
Figueiredo and Garcia
Fernandes, circa 1520.

Background image:
This figure, a cosmographer
or pilot, is lost in thought
over an amillary sphere and
an astronomical table.
Excerpt from the Evora
Guia Náutico (Nautical
Guide), one of the two
oldest printed Portuguese
nautical documents (circa
1516).

foot on it, I gathered these plants which I offer to Your Grace and that, in this realm we shall call Saint Mary roses." These were roses of Jericho, small shrubs that might as well have been brought back from the moon.

Henry instantly ordered Afonso Gonçalves Baldaia, another squire, to return with Gil Eanes to push farther into this unknown world. "They traveled fifty leagues past the cape, where they found a land with no houses, but saw footprints of men and camels."

Two years later, Afonso Gonçalves Baldaia left again for the south and landed at what he believed to be the mouth of a river; he called it Rio de Ouro, the river of gold. Heitor Homem and Diogo Lopes, two highborn young men, galloped on horseback into this unexplored land. "And so that neither they nor their horses would tire, he ordered that they take no defensive weapons, but only their lances and swords to attack if necessary. For if they met people who wanted to take them, their best defense would be the hooves of their horses, unless they found a single man they could capture without risk. And these young men demonstrated the type of men they would one day become as they accomplished this task. For although they were far from their country and they did not know what type or how many people they would find, not to mention the fear of wild beasts whose frightening appearance could have troubled the minds of such youth who were barely seventeen years old, they did not hesitate over any of these things, and set out with great courage and rode upstream for a distance of seven leagues." They did, in fact, fight a group of natives.

The essential factor in these discovery voyages was not the compass, which still served no great purpose, or the caravel, which had not yet been modified to replace the *barinel* or the *barcha* (small sailing ships fitted with oars), but rather, breaking the psychological barrier of the Atlantic Ocean which, beyond Europe, was still known as the *Mare Oceanum*, a sea that led nowhere.

OTHER STARS

With each year, the Portuguese continued farther south down the west coast of Africa, surprised with the enormous size of the continent. The first economic benefits of this undertaking were the slaves taken from the land of the Moors. They were sold in Lagos, the Portuguese port where ships were fitted for Africa, then in Lisbon, where the Casa da Guiné, or House of Guinea, was set up in the mid-fifteenth century. This was renamed the House of Elmina when the fort of Elmina was created in 1481, in the heart of the land where the explorers had found gold.

Around this time, the Portuguese altered the design of their ships, making it easier for them to sail against the trade winds and harmattan winds on the return trip to Lagos. Sailors also took advantage of the west winds in the mid-Atlantic.

The first direct contact between the West and the overseas territories, with the exception of Marco Polo's voyages, started in the Gulf of Guinea. The Portuguese discovered bronzes in Benin, and African artists portrayed these unusual visitors whose clothes and firearms were extremely exotic. Bronze plates (lost-wax process). Benin, sixteenth-seventeenth centuries.

Left:
Warriors and musicians.

Right:
Bearded and long-haired Portuguese man bearing a firearm.

With the invention of the *volte*, the caravels sailed far into the high seas; more sophisticated navigational techniques included the compass and astronomical navigation by means of the polar star. As they pushed down the coast, the Portuguese marked their passage by setting up *padroes*, initially wooden crosses, then stones, which marked the limit reached by each new expedition. Meanwhile, they were acquiring an enormous amount of information, expanding on the ancient and medieval knowledge of the world.

One of the first surprises encountered by natural historians was the baobab tree (named three centuries later by the French botanist Michel Adanson), one among tens of thousands of samples of hitherto unknown vegetation, insects, and animals brought back to Europe. The Portuguese were astonished at the size of this tree, which they first discovered on Goree Island off the coast of Dakar, where a large expedition force under the command of Lançarote de Ilha had anchored. According to this knight: "They found extremely large, strange-looking trees, among which there was one that measured one hundred and eight spans around the base."

A dozen years later, Alvise Ca' da Mosto, a Venetian adventurer and merchant on a trading trip to Gambia, reported that a riverbank, "was filled with the trees with wonderfully thick trunks that abound in this land. Concerning the size of these trees, I will provide a single example: once, when we were drawing water from a fountain near the banks of the river, we discovered an immense and extremely wide tree, whose circumference was no less than its height; we estimated that it was twenty paces high and measured seventeen paces around the base of the trunk."

This traveler was curious about everything he saw. "I deduced that the native people ate elephant meat, and I had a piece of it cut and taken to my ship. I ate it boiled and grilled, to try something new and to be able to brag that I had tasted a meat that no other Venetian has ever yet tasted. I found it tough and tasteless. I also took one of its feet and part of its trunk aboard my ship, and I pulled out several hairs from its body. These were black, one and a half times the size of my palm and fairly thick. Like any other piece of meat, I had it salted, then presented it in Spain to the Infante Dom Henrique of Portugal, who

received it as a great gift, as these were the first things he had seen from this country and also because he wanted to own these strange objects, which had come from distant lands discovered on his initiative and thanks to his perseverance."

During his two voyages to Guinea in the mid-fifteenth century, Ca' de Mosto was interested in more than just exotic natural history specimens. He also brought back one of the first records of the southern skies, and was the first in the Atlantic Ocean to describe the Southern Cross. "During our trip to the mouth of the [Gambia] river, we only saw the north star once, appearing very low on the horizon. We could only see it in calm, clear weather and even so, it appeared at a height of one lance above the sea. We also saw six large, bright stars, low over the sea, which we used as a landmark. They were arranged in the south in this pattern:

*

*   ***

*

We thought we could recognize the big dipper, but we could not see the main star, which cannot reasonably be so." Indeed, this was the Southern Cross, the stars at the opposite pole, "which no one from our earliest ancestors had ever seen," according to Dante. Dante had celebrated their beauty without ever seeing them either, on the basis of descriptions provided by overland travelers on the silk routes. "The sky seemed to dance by their lights. How you are widowed, Septentrion, as you are deprived of this show." As for Ca' da Mosto, he was somewhat worried about losing sight of the pole star, an ancient navigational guide, and also the only point that could be used to measure latitude and determine the position of the ships along the apparently endless African coast.

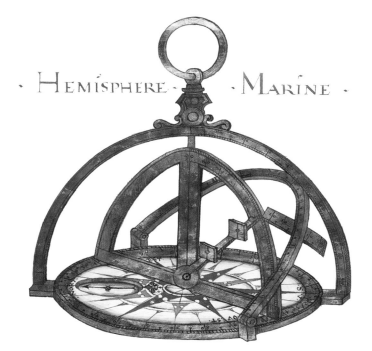

· HEMISPHERE · · MARINE ·

VI MENSIVM EST
T V M P E R T O T V M
A R T I C V S
ENTALIS
CANCRI
CIDENTALIS
Pont Euxinus
Libia deserta
Æthiopia per totu
Indicum pelagus
Sinus Gangeticus
Linea equinoctialis
A P R I C O R N I
MARE PRASSODVM
TERRA VEL MARE INCOGNITVM
A N T A R T I C V S
T V M P E R T O T V M
VI MENSIVM

Cape of Storms

Shortly after becoming king, John II of Portugal rejected a proposal by the Geneose sailor Christopher Columbus in 1484 to support an expedition to the Indies via a westward route. He may have been interested, but his refusal was based on psychological and practical grounds. The new king of Portugal wanted to pursue the course begun by Henry the Navigator in Sagres under John I and which continued with the reigns of Edward and Alfonso V, his father.

A new expedition ordered to sail around the immense continent of Africa was organized under the command of Bartolomeu Dias, who had been a superintendent in the royal warehouses. The small fleet left Lisbon at the end of August 1487. No original written report remains from this voyage. The ships rounded the southern tip of Africa, weathering the rough seas of the South Atlantic, without ever catching sight of land. "When the storm finally died out, Bartolomeu Dias steered an eastward course, believing that the coast was still following a north-south direction. Yet after sailing for several days without any sign of land, he turned north and reached a bay, which he called Vacca (cows), as he sighted many of these animals in the fields, guarded by shepherds."

Cape Vacca is situated in South Africa at longitude 22° E. Somewhere in the vicinity of present-day Port Elizabeth, Dias met with his captains and crew, who refused to continue on toward the Indian Ocean. Dias set up his *padrao* at 27° E. On the return trip, he named the final headland Cape of Storms. King John II renamed it the Cape of Good Hope, "as it opened the route to India that had been much-coveted and highly sought with such persistence for so long."

Luis de Camoès, the Homeric poet, wrote *The Lusciads,* an epic work extolling the Portuguese discoveries. In the fifth canto, he wrote of a prophecy by Adamastor, a giant who guarded the route to India: "I am the immense and mysterious cape that you call the Cape of Storms, as I have revealed myself to Ptolemy, Pomponius, Strabo, Pliny, and all other ancients. I end the African coast by this headland stretching toward the Antarctic pole, and that your courage transgresses. Heed the misfortunes that will be inflicted for your excessive daring on the sea and lands that you conquest. Know that the uncontrollable storms and winds shall render this access deadly to any ships impudent enough to once again attempt this voyage. I shall inflict on the first fleet to round these untamed waters a punishment so sudden that they will feel the terrible consequences before they have even perceived any danger." Camoès drew his inspiration for this passage from a dramatic event that occurred during the Lusitanian era. In 1500, a gale in the stretch of water off Tristan da Cunha Island devastated the fleet that had been sent out to settle the Indian Empire, the first victims in history of what would become known as the "roaring forties." Bartolomeu Dias died in this naval disaster without ever again rounding the cape he discovered.

Map of the area around the Cape of Good Hope, decorated with *padroes*, or stones, marking the continual Portuguese expansion along the African coast.
Portulan du Roteiro by Francisco de Roís, pilot with the fleet of António de Miranda Azevedo, who set up Portuguese colonies in the Molucca Islands (Spice Islands) in 1513-1516.

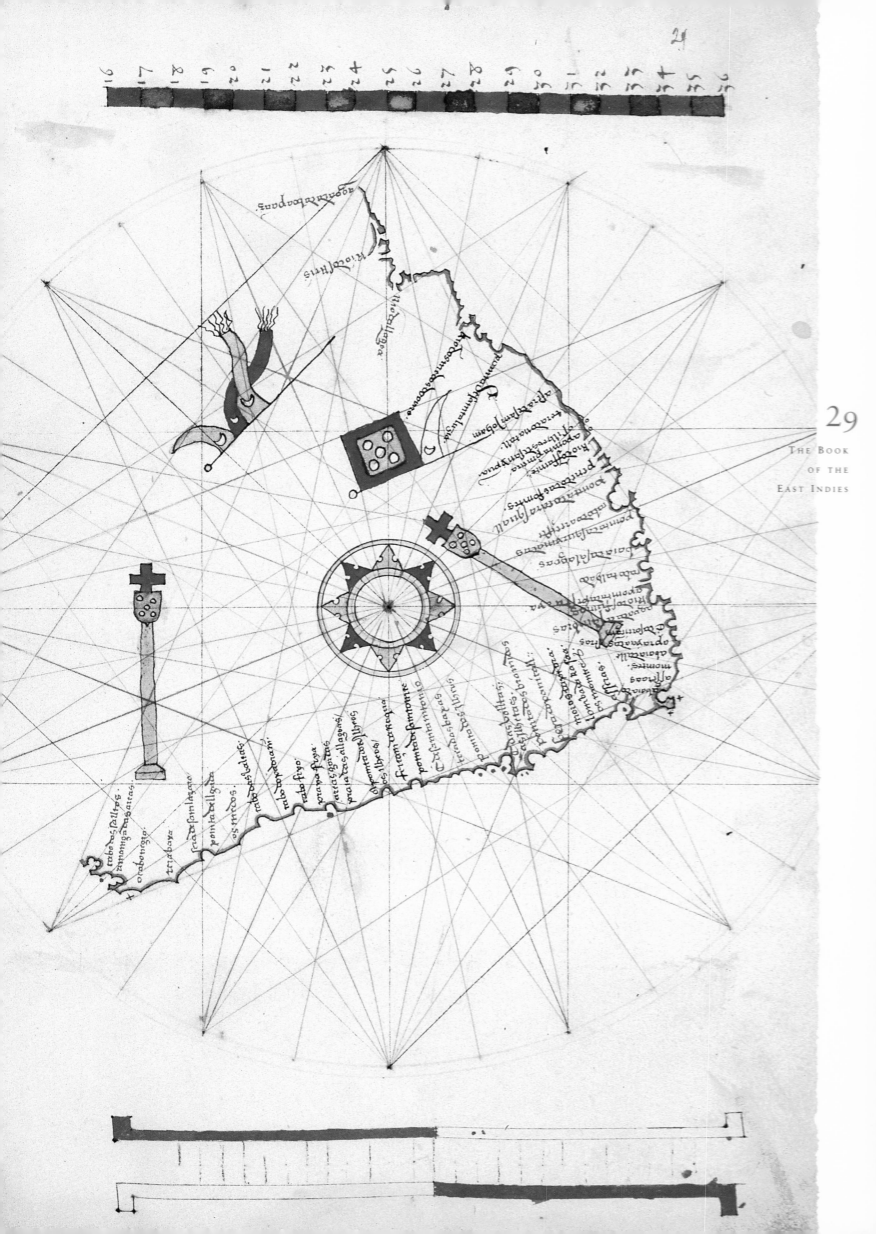

On the Right Track

King Manuel I (nicknamed "the Fortunate" for the many profitable undertakings he inherited) disregarded the advice of many people concerned with the conquest of the East Indies. Instead, in deference to the wishes of Henry the Navigator and the unfulfilled hopes of John II, in 1496 he asked Vasco da Gama, a gentleman from his household, to command a new fleet to be sent out to discover the sea route to India. In the oath pronounced by the *capitào mor,* the arrogance and solemnity of the terms match the scope of the mission and the ruthless energy of the king's designated commander in chief.

"I, Vasco da Gama, who, in obeying your orders, my extremely powerful King in the highest, my Lord, will now leave to discover the seas and lands of the East. I solemnly swear by the sign of this cross on which my hand is placed, that, in the service of God and in your service, I shall always maintain this standard unfurled, never folded, in the face of the Moors, the gentiles, and any other people I shall meet along my way. And I swear that through all the perils of water, fire, or iron, always I will keep this cross and shall defend it to the death. Furthermore, I swear that throughout this undertaking of discovery upon which you are sending me, I shall serve you with loyalty, vigilance, courage, and faith, honoring your orders and obeying your instructions. And I shall continue until the day when, God willing, I return to Your Highness."

The small fleet numbered four ships; the two largest were barely over one hundred tons burden. They set sail on July 8, 1497, the day of the Virgin, from Restelo beach downstream from Lisbon, not far from the present-day site of the Tower of Belém. This area also became known as the "Beach of Tears" during the *Carreira da India,* when ships plied the sea route to India.

Joao de Barros, writing in the mid-sixteenth century in his *Décadas,* described the departure of the expedition. "When it came time to set sail, the brothers from the hermitage and a few priests, who had come from the city to perform Mass, organized an extremely pious procession that took place in the following order: first the brothers and priests, then Vasco da Gama and the other ship captains and chief officers of the fleet, all holding a lit candle in their hands; next came crowds of people from the city, responding to the litanies chanted by the priests and brothers, who were leading the procession. They walked in this way to the longboats which were to transport Vasco da Gama and his crew to the ships. The crowd fell silent and everyone fell to their knees, while the vicar of the hermitage pronounced a general confession. He then gave absolution to all those who were leaving, in accordance with bulls obtained earlier from the Holy See by the Infant Dom Henrique for all those who would die during these discoveries and these conquests. There were many tears at this moment; it was almost as if this beach has taken possession of all the tears, so

Background image:
Vasco da Gama. Wood
engraving from an ink wash
drawing by Gaspar Correia
for the manuscript of
the second volume of his
Lendas da India (Legends
of India). Mid-sixteenth
century (after 1540).

Right:
A fleet sets sail. Illuminated
manuscript for volume
four of Além-Douro in
the *Leitura Nova* series by
D. Manuel.
Mid-sixteenth century.
Sixty lavishly illuminated
volumes formed the
Leitura Nova series; this
collection grew with each
year, with the inclusion of
official Portuguese texts
and major governmental
decisions, under the
personal responsibility of
the guardian of the royal
archives.

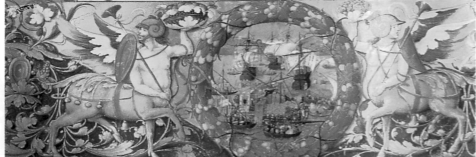

many of which have since been shed, now that fleets set out each year for the
distant countries that Vasco da Gama was preparing to discover. And when it
came time to unfurl the sails, and when the sailors, as is their custom, cheered
gaily for their journey to begin by shouting "Bon voyage! Bon voyage!," the cries
of those left behind on shore increased. These people began to commend these
voyagers to God and to speak among themselves, exchanging words on the
sentiments that so upset them."

The fleet set sail via the *volte*, using the favorable winds as far as South
Africa, which they reached after four months of sailing. Slowly, the ships, which
kept filling up with water, made their way south as the nights grew longer. They
rounded the Cape of Good Hope on November 22, after four and a half months
at sea. Battling an opposing current, in an exhausting cycle of calm spells and
strong winds, the ships then slowly veered toward the northeast.

"Vasco da Gama, seeing that the crew was urging him to turn back,
immediately responded that, in the depths of his heart, he had promised God
that he would not retreat a single span of the route already sailed and that he
would have the first sailor who spoke of it again thrown overboard. Hence,
these desperate men continued their route in the wide open seas, and the storms
grew more violent. The wind had started to rage, and it changed directions so
often that the sailors no longer knew which way it was blowing; and sometimes
it died down totally and left the ships stranded among the waves, battering the
ships as they pleased... And the men tied themselves to the ships with ropes so
that they wouldn't fall, as everything in these ships was breaking into pieces; and
they cried and pleaded, imploring God's mercy... And the wind, which had died

Por quanto vos don Juan de Guzman duque de medina sidonia my primo e del my
conselo me aveys otras vezes fablado diziendo que çierta tierra que agora de nuevo mandas-
tes descobrir allende de la mar e el traves delas Canarias que dezis ques ...
de el cabo de aguer hasta la tierra alta y al cabo de bojador con dos Rios en...
termino de uno llamado la mar pequeña donde ay muchas pesquerias e...
puede aprovechar la tierra adentro e y o me suplicastes e pedistes por m...
vos hiziese m(erce)d de todo ello por que esto aumentar e tenerlo vos dezis que ser...
mi servido o Como mas my m(erce)d fuese e yo acatando los muchos e leales
servicios que vos del dicho duque me aveys fecho e fazeys continuo e fare...
de aqui adelante tovelo por bien por ende por la presente vos ta...
m(erce)d a vos el dicho duque de toda la dicha mar e tierra desde el cabo de aguer
hasta la tierra alta e cabo de bojador con todos los Rios e pesquerias e te...
tierra adentro e los puertos e todos los otros derechos e pechos...
la justicia e jurisdiçion alta e baxa mero mixto ynperio e con todo lo...
mas que en ello es a mi pertenescen e al señorio e corona Real de sus my...
...e finando que a mi e para los Reyes que despues de mi vinieren...
...me dieron e me hizieron de oro e plata e otros metales hago...
e donaçion vos hago e doy que sea b(ie)n por juz e h(ere)dad que sean...
jamas para vos e que otros herederos e sus sesores los que vos obieredes...
...e heredar en q... y tener vos lo sobredicha m(erce)d e otorgo por q... yo
como Rey y señor no reconosciente en lo temporal supieron e de... p...
mote... cierta açiençia e poderio Real absoluto vos hago esta dicha m...
donaçion de toda la dicha mar e tierra e playas e cabos de aguer...
jador e tierra firme con las pesquerias delos Rios e con todo lo que dicho...
es y por la presente vos doy my poder... que tomedes la posesion...
... corporal e natural de todo ello e mando que vos den e entre...
dadas mis cartas patentes e previllejos delo suso dicho...
...e... e mando que obedezcan e q... la m(erce)d por esta my çedula.
... y para las dar e... mando... otro por...
en Valladolid a otho dias de Jullio año del naçimiento de ... mill e quatro...

Left:
Manuscript page reporting
Vasco da Gama's voyage,
attributed to Alvaro Velho.

Below:
The Lisbon castle and
cathedral, before the
1755 earthquake.
The city's harbor along
the Tagus River looked
much as it did during the
age of the great navigators.
Azulejo from the Ordem
Terceira da Panitência
do Seráfico Padre Sào
Francisco monastery, at
Salvador de Bahia (Brazil).
First half of the eighteenth
century.

down for a moment, suddenly whipped up again and blew even more violently than before, and the men were exhausted from operating the pumps, as the ships were taking in water from all sides. These men had no rest for either their bodies or souls, and they started to become ill and die of fatigue. They implored the captains to return to the coast, but they continued to reply that they would only do as Vasco da Gama so commanded. And Vasco da Gama answered the pleas of his sailors with strong hard words: that he had already told them that he would not retreat a single span, even if he saw death one hundred times before his eyes, as this was the promise he had made to Our Lord; also that he would not permit them—through lack of faith and weakness—to lose everything they had achieved to that point; and that he ordered them to remember that they had rounded the Cape, and that they would soon land on the shores of India, which they had come to discover."

The story (*Legends of India*) by Gaspar Correia, a chronicler from the mid-sixteenth century, is a somewhat fictionalized account, but it is similar to descriptions of navigational conditions prevalent throughout the winter in the southern hemisphere off the Cape of Good Hope. Tomé Lopes, for example, writing aboard a ship in Estêvào da Gama's fleet that set sail from Lisbon in 1502, penned the following description: "On Tuesday, June 7, during the night shift, we were assaulted by a storm driven by a west wind that was so violent, the ships were separated one from another, and in the morning, only two were together, the *Júlia* and us. And we didn't know what direction the others had gone. In the final night shift, just before daylight, we no longer had a studding sail: we only had a very small low sail. During the third squall, the wind was so strong that it broke our lateen yard in the middle and broke the *Júlia's* mast, which frightened us all greatly. That day and the following night, we ran under

bare masts, and we put up the small sail on the foremast. The heavy sea, the immense waves crashing upon us, were astonishing things to see. That day, we all made many vows, and we drew straws to choose those who would visit the church, Notre-Dame-Sainte-Marie de Guadalupe." This was a sanctuary in Estremadura, famous among sailors from the Iberian peninsula.

This phase of the journey was certainly difficult for Vasco da Gama's crew; indeed, Bartholomeu Dias' own sailors had given up at this point. Some records note the early stirrings of a mutiny, but they differ when it occurred, either on the outbound or inbound trip. In any case, the boats sailed on.

The ships sighted landfall on Christmas Day, calling it Natal, the name by which it is still known. On January 24, 1498, the fleet anchored at the mouth of the Zambezi River to replenish their water supplies, careen the ships, and repair the damage caused by the storms. The river was named Rio dos Bòns Sinais, the River of Good Auspices. Scurvy had broken out. "Many of our men fell ill at this place; their hands and feet swelled up, their gums were so inflamed that they had swollen over their teeth, so that they couldn't eat."

On March 1, the Portuguese discovered Mozambique. "The men of the land are copper-colored, well-built, and follow of the religion of Mohammed. They speak the language of the Moors. Their clothes are made of fine cotton and linen fabric with many brightly colored and richly embroidered stripes. Everyone wears a turban, edged with silk and embroidered with gold thread. They are traders and do business with the white Moors, including four ships that were anchored at port and loaded with gold, silver, fabrics, nutmeg, pepper, ginger, silver rings adorned with many pearls, seed pearls, and rubies— things also worn by the men of this country. It appeared to us, according to what they told us, that all these things had been imported, that it was the Moors who brought them, except for the gold; and that farther on, in the direction we were heading, there was more. Stones, seed pearls, and spices were so abundant, they said, that it wasn't even necessary to barter for them: you could gather them by the basketful. A sailor who was with the commander understood all of this: he had been a prisoner of the Moors and therefore had spoken to those we found there."

They also received news of Prester John, the legendary Christian priest-king, an idealized image of the Negus, or leader, whose kingdom was said to be somewhere near Abyssinia. These signs confirmed that they were nearing their goal. Without understanding why, the sick sailors recovered their health during a stop at Mombassa, where they almost fell into a trap. On April 14, they dropped anchor at Malindi (Kenya). Gifts were exchanged with the king, but the most important gift that Vasco da Gama received was an Indian pilot, a Moor from Gujarat (a region of India near the Indus) sent by the king to lead the Portuguese straight to Calicut.

Background image:
Nutmeg plant (*Myristica fragrans*). The nutmeg nut grew exclusively in the miniscule Banda Islands, in the Molucca Archipelago. Wood engraving from the *Tratado de las Drogas y Medicinas de las Indias Orientales* by Cristovào da Costa, 1578.

Right:
Map showing a bird's eye view of Mozambique, in one of the manuscript charts drawn up by D. Joáo de Castro. If the Portuguese ships arrived in the region too late to pick up the southwest winds that would carry them to Goa, they would put into port on the island, where they sometimes waited up to eight months until the summer monsoon began. Mozambique was a charnel house, due to the tropical illnesses that could wipe out up to half of a ship's crew while they wintered in the harbor.
D. Joáo de Castro, *Roteiro de Viagem de Lisboa a Goa* (Travel charts from Lisbon to Goa), 1538.

ESTAEARMADACÕQVE LESNACOSTADARABIAIV

SERAS

MASCATE

ILHEO

DOMFERNÃDOTOMOVASGA
MTODEMASCATEOANODESSS

ANTONIODEVALA
DARES

MANOELDE
MELO

NICOLAVDE
CRASTO

JORGEDEMO
VRA

DOMFERNÃDOD
EMOROI

DOMGERONIMODE
CASTELOBRÃÇO

BOMMA
OELMASC
RENHÃS

DOMALVO
RODETA
IDE

GUMESDASIL
VA

GOMÇALO
LCAM

DOMALVORODASILV

Preceding double page:
Portuguese fleet at Muscat
(Oman) in 1955. The
Portuguese took control of
the Red Sea, the Persian
Gulf, and the Arabian Sea
as soon as they arrived
in the Indian Ocean.
They managed to stop the
Arab sea trade by setting
up forts in Ormuz and
Muscat, and by posting
their corsairs at key sea
traffic points in the Oman
Sea. *Le Livro de Lisuarte de
Abreu* (circa 1558-1564).

Background image:
Pepper. Wood engraving
from the *Tratado de las
Drogas y Medicinas de las
Indias Orientales* by
Cristovào da Costa, 1578.

Left:
Portuguese ships.
Seventeenth-century carpet.
Persian art.

Right:
Bird's eye view of Calicut.
The Portuguese set up
their first trading
companies in Calicut and
Cochin on the Malabar
coast. The Calicut fortress
was built from 1512
to 1525, as it was
important to protect the
Portuguese settlement
from hostile Muslims.
Manuscript of *Lendas
da India* (Legends of India),
1550-1563, by the
chronicler Gaspar Correia.

WHO LED YOU HERE?

"On Friday, which was the 18th of May, after we had been at sea twenty-three days, we discovered a high coastline. Throughout all these days, we sailed before the wind, so that we must have traveled at least six hundred leagues during this crossing. At the time we sighted land, we were about eight leagues from it. We threw out the sounding lead and were then in forty-five fathoms. That night, we set sail toward the southwest to stay away from the coast. The next day (May 19), we returned to find it, but we did not get close enough for the pilot to exactly identify the coast. This was due to the large number of storms and downpours that we experienced in this land during our crossing and along the coast we were nearing."

This was the beginning of the monsoon season in the southwest, which would soon make any navigation along the Malabar coast dangerous.

"On Sunday (May 20), we were near large mountains, the highest that the men had ever seen, which towered over the city of Calicut [Kozhikode], and we came near enough so that the pilot leading us could recognize them. He told us that this was the land that we were seeking. The evening of this same day, we anchored two leagues below of this city of Calicut, because the pilot had taken another town, called Capua, for Calicut. And farther below this city was another, called Pandarane. We dropped anchor along the coast, approximately one and a half leagues out to sea." The pilot probably did not make a mistake, but had guided the ships to a better mooring ground.

Several days later, on the advice of the rajah of Calicut, Vasco da Gama would moor his ship at Pandarane, north of Calicut, but "below" in relation to the wind, as indicated in the logs. Pandarane was the only port safe enough to shelter the ships during the monsoon season, due to an odd phenomenon by which it was protected from the heavy swells from the west that battered the coast. Without this information, Vasco da Gama's mission, which had been prepared without any knowledge of the monsoon season, might have failed, as he would not have been able to anchor his ships and disembark, given that all the harbors along the Malabar coast were inaccessible and closed to navigation during the summer.

On May 21, a conversation was held between a Portuguese emissary, a prisoner brought along to perform dangerous missions in exchange for his freedom, and the Indians, through the intermediary of two Moors from Tunis, who spoke Castilian and Genoese. Alvaro Velho noted the exact words of the brief dialogue.

"To the devil with you! Who led you here? What are you seeking so far away?"

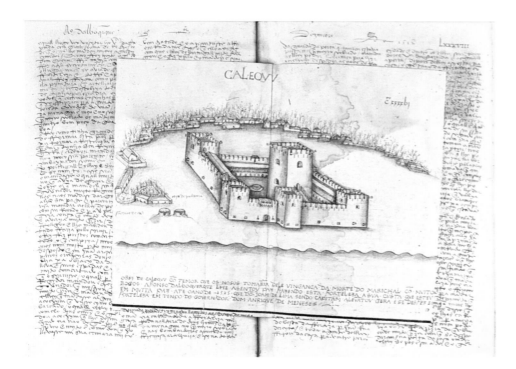

man ten se de rrou bar he ni so
bam_ sam m̃ valen tes homes
grandes caual guadores he f
sua ley he de Jin tios ꝫ.

"The inhabitants of the kingdom of Cambay are accomplished horsemen and archers." The city of Cambay (Khambhat) in the Gujurat, north of Bombay, was the starting point for expeditions inland in northern India during the Age of Discovery.

Left:
Horsemen from the kingdom of Cambay.

Right:
A Portuguese man sheltered under an umbrella held by a servant.
Anonymous Portuguese manuscript, mid-sixteenth century. *Codex Casanatense.*

Following page:
This nativity scene, attributed to António de Holanda, dates from the first quarter of the sixteenth century.
In addition to the symbol of the three wise men bearing their precious gifts, the work also includes images of Indian pearls and rubies and gold coins struck by various Portuguese sovereigns.
In the foreground, the prestigious D. Manuel *português*, worth ten cruzados.
Illuminated manuscript from the D. Manuel Book of Hours (circa 1517-1538).

"We have come to convert Muslims to Christianity and to find spices."

This first exchange on the coastline of India summed up the annoyance of the Islamic communities of sea traders; the monopoly they shared with the Venetians on either side of the Arabian Sea was suddenly threatened. The exchange also reflects the ambiguous nature of these discoveries, which threw together missionaries on a quest for lost souls and merchants seeking immense treasures.

"They then said: 'Why does the king of Castille, the king of France, and the seigniory of Venice not send anyone here?' He replied that the king of Portugal did not consent to do so. And they told him he was right. And they then welcomed him and gave him bread and honey to eat."

The Portuguese encountered several surprises, beginning with the unusual decor of the Hindu temples, which they took to be churches. "This city of Calicut is inhabited by Christians... They then took us to a large church. Inside, there was a small image that they said was of Our Lady. And in front of the main door of the church, along the wall, were seven small bells. Here the commander prayed, and we along with him... Many other saints were painted on the walls of the church, and they wore diadems. These paintings were different from our own, as their teeth were so large that they extended beyond the mouth the length of a thumb, and each saint had four or five arms."

The greatest surprise to the Portuguese, however—exhausted by nearly one year at sea—came when they noticed that no one was overly impressed with their arrival. "The next morning, which was Monday May 28, the captain went to speak to the king, and he took with him thirteen of his men. I was one of them. We were all wearing our most handsome clothes. We were carrying on our launches many bombards, trumpets, and flags." The troupe headed off from Pandarane toward Calicut.

The interview with the *samuttiri*, the "lord of the sea" in Malayalam, which the Portuguese transformed into *samorin*, was as cordial and as distant as Indian protocol would allow. The commander thought it a good idea to have them believe his king was immensely wealthy. The *samorin* replied that this king was his brother and that he would send ambassadors.

After that, he looked at the captain, who was
seated opposite, and told him to talk to the men
who accompanied him, as they were very important
people: the captain could say what he wanted,
and he would transmit the message to them.
The captain answered that he was an ambassador
from the king of Portugal and that he was bearing
a message that could only be delivered directly
to him. The king said that this was very good,
and the captain was led into a room. When he was
there, the king stood up and entered the room
where the captain had been led, while we remained
at the place I mentioned. When he was near
the captain, the king lay down on another daybed,
upholstered in fabric with gold embroidery,
and asked what he wanted. The captain answered
that he was an ambassador from the king of
Portugal, who was a lord of many lands and was
rich in all things. Much richer than any other king
in these regions; and that for sixty years, the kings
that had preceded him had sent ships every
year to explore these regions, as they knew that
there were kings here that were Christians like
himself. This is why they had this country
discovered, not because they needed gold or silver;
as they already had so much of their own, they had
no need to get it in this country.

Alvaro Velho, aboard the *Sào Rafael*,
believed to have written Vasco da Gama's log,
May 28, 1498.

este Rey de canbaya
he ho que pos çerco ha
fortaleza dedio he
esta tirado pelo na
tural.

The next day, Vasco da Gama prepared gifts. "On Tuesday, the commander had the following presents prepared for the king: twelve *lambéis* (striped Moorish fabric), four scarlet hoods, six hats, four coral necklaces, a six-piece service of bowls, a crate of sugar, and four barrels, two filled with oil and two with honey. According to the local custom, no object could be presented to the king unless it had first been seen by the Moor, who worked as his messenger, as well as by the *bale* (the *báli*, or governor). The commander therefore informed these men of his gifts. They arrived to inspect them and started to mock these presents. They said that this was nothing to offer a king, that the poorest of traders arriving from Mecca or the Indies gave him greater gifts, and that if he wanted to give him a gift, he must send gold, as the king would not accept any of the items he had prepared. The commander was saddened by these words. He said he had not brought gold, and furthermore, that he was not a trader, but an ambassador, that he would give him what he had brought, and that these were his gifts and not those of the king. The king of Portugal would later send presents, and he would send many other, much more valuable things. If the *samorin* did not want them, he would send them back to the ships. They replied that they would not take these items to the king, and they would not allow anyone else to take them to the king. When they left, we saw certain Moorish traders arrive, and they treated the presents the commander wanted to send to the king with disdain."

The miserable lot of Portuguese goods, viewed in the context of the fabulous silk market, made Vasco da Gama and his men look like half-starved sea traders and buccaneers. They were unaware of others who, like Saint Thomas's

Christians, had already created Jewish and Christian settlements on the India coast with the aim of trading pepper—although they were replaced by Arab merchants once Islam started to spread. The Indians, situated at the heart of the trading activity, had little to learn regarding navigation and everything to teach the Portuguese about business in their land. Yet the Moors were mistaken to mock these new arrivals.

GOA

Worried about the increasing numbers of Arab ships, and observing that tension was starting to poison his relationship with the *samorin*, Vasco da Gama set sail from Calicut on August 29, without waiting for the northeast winds of mid-December, which would have been favorable to his return voyage. The crossing to Lisbon was extremely difficult and slow. Several dozen men died, including Vasco da Gama's brother Paulo, whose body was buried on the Azores instead of being simply thrown to sea, as was the custom. The pumps could barely keep the two remaining ships afloat as they sat at anchor in the archipelago, returning from the two-year trip.

A captain who had stopped at Terceira, where they had put into port, rushed back to Lisbon to announce the return of the expedition and to collect the reward granted to bearers of good tidings. "Arthur Rodrigues, who knew that the king was at Sintra, immediately went there. He arrived in the evening. The king had just sat down for supper. He was led to the king and, kissing his hand, said to him: 'My Lord, I kiss the hand of your highness to thank him for the reward that he will give me for the great news I bring. I left Terceira four days ago, just as two ships had anchored. They had arrived from India...' The king did not want to hear another word. Rising immediately from the table, he went to the palace chapel where he prayed for many long hours. The news spread quickly; all members of the court rushed to the Sintra palace to congratulate the king and share their joy with him. The king immediately made Arthur Rodrigues a gentleman in his household and his son a pageboy, and he gave him one hundred golden cruzados. He announced that he would leave for Lisbon the following morning, as he knew that other ships arriving from Terceira would bring more detailed news.

"The king's impatience grew as more information arrived. He sent several boats to the mouth of the Tagus River, to await the vessels from India... Bedecked with flags, the ships finally sailed into the port of Lisbon. The king was waiting in the Casa da Mina, which was renamed Casa da India, in honor of this event. When the ships dropped anchor, they saluted the city by firing their guns." Vasco da Gama was looking proud, with a beard he had grown during the trip, as he jumped onto the sands at Restelo and came to kneel before his king.

ARMADA DECAPITAĪSQVEV

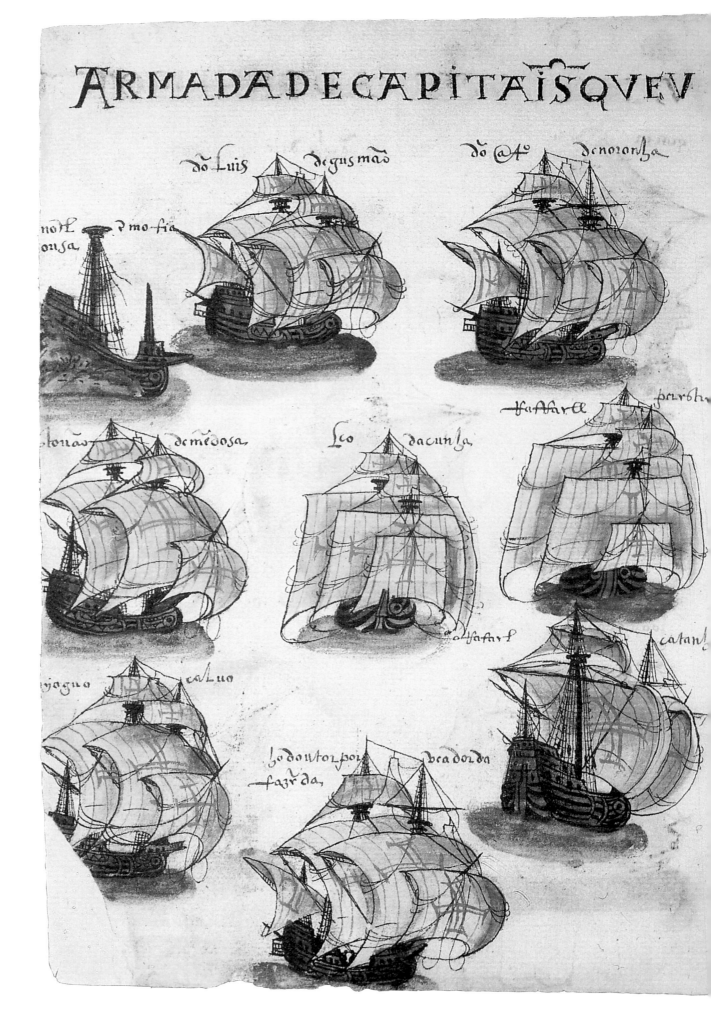

The Portuguese had acquired the cargo at Calicut—despite the difficulty they had selling their unappreciated goods in India. After such a long voyage, the cargo was still immensely profitable. "When the ships were unloaded, the king told Dom Vasco to pay his men... The pepper and all the spices were weighed, and the king had his officers draw up an account of all the expenses for the ships, the goods, and other necessary items they had taken with them, as well as the payment and rewards for the captains and all men aboard. And, comparing the total of all these expenses with that of the value of the goods brought back, they found that for each hundred spent, they had earned six hundred." All the members of the expedition received bonuses, while privileges, gifts, and pensions were heaped on the captain. Dom Vasco was ennobled to Count of Vidigueira and named commander general of the Indian fleets.

Preceding double page:
The fleet commanded by
Diogo Lopes de Sequeira
in 1519. This naval
expedition sailed to the
Red Sea and captured
Massawa.
Livro de Lisuarte de Abreu
(circa 1558-1564).

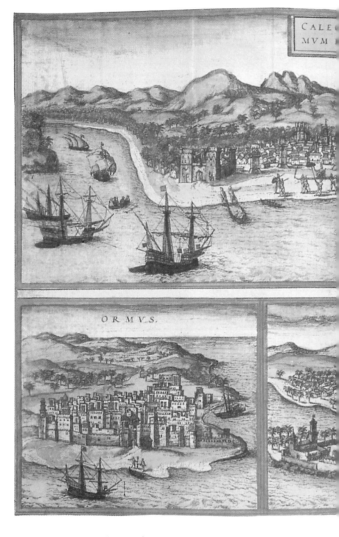

Dom Manuel immediately informed the Catholic monarchs. "The ships that we sent two years ago have found and discovered India and other nearby realms; they have penetrated and sailed through a sea where they found great cities, with tall wealthy buildings, and densely populated cities, where the trade in spices and precious stones takes place." Dom Manuel, writing this report at a time when a violent controversy was swirling around Columbus, whose disgrace was imminent, gave Portugal an immediate lead in the race to the Indies.

During this period, a merchant named Girolamo Sernigi, who worked in a Lisbon trading house, wrote a long letter to a Florentine correspondent, in which he made several subtle and shrewd observations. "It is a magnificent feat, and this king of Portugal deserves praise from all of Christendom. But he must be very careful in the future... This is why I say that the sultan, these kings, and these Moors will do everything in their power to keep the king of Portugal out of this trade. If the king of Portugal continues, he could indeed sell spices at Porto Pisano (the port of Pisa), at prices far lower than they cost in Cairo, as he can bring them back at a far lesser cost. And we could be forced to call back the Venetian and Genoese merchants, as well as those from other nations. They will sorely miss the revenues, as they are chiefly produced from the trade between Syria and us. This is why I am certain they will do anything to ruin this voyage, but they will have to work very hard to do so."

Vasco da Gama died at Cochin on Christmas Day 1524, after working for the government for several months, where he earned respect and fear for his merciless authority. The Portuguese empire was formed in just a dozen years. Afonso de Albuquerque conceived of the plan to set up Portuguese strongholds in strategic points in the India Ocean. The commanders received clear orders concerning their conduct. "If Pedro Alvares Cabral does not manage to obtain the friendship and proof of loyalty from the *samorin* of Calicut, he should declare war and then pursue it." As for converting the local people to Christianity, "if these people are so determined to follow their errors, by refusing to accept the words of the truth Faith, denying the law of peace that must unite men and exist among them to conserve the human race, and creating obstacles and hindrances to the exercise of trade and exchange, we must then, by fire and sword, wage a cruel war. The captains have abundant and clear instructions on all these points."

Views of Calicut, Ormuz, Cannanore and Elmina. These were key sites in the Portuguese East India empire in the late sixteenth century.
Civitates Orbis Terrarum, a six-volume atlas by Georg Braun. Frans Hogenberg (1572-1618).

The Portuguese court held out great hopes in the civilizing force of free trade among primitive populations. It had worked fairly well in Africa, but the situation was obviously very different in the Indian Ocean. The instructions were applied to the letter, because, as expected, the Portuguese were poorly received; they had no scruples about cruel retaliation.

Goa was occupied and fortified in 1510. Portugal was proudly setting up its empire in the Indian territory. Dom Manuel was nicknamed—not without a certain tinge of envy—"the pepper king," and his ships returned to Europe with other cargo besides spices. Exotic Goa, capital of the viceroy, the "Rome of the Orient," tarnished the glory of Venice, tucked away in the Adriatic Sea.

The "blue-eyed bearded men" who landed in Canton in 1516 obtained the concession for Macao in 1533. Macao's Saint Paul Church was the most modern Christian building in Asia at the time.

In 1542, three Portuguese adventurers landed at Tanegashima, a small island near Kyushu. Portugal had reached Cipango. Tea was described in 1570 by the monk Gaspar da Cruz as an unpleasant beverage, but one that was important from a protocol point of view. "For anyone who arrives at the home of an important man, it is customary to offer a porcelain cup on an elegant tray to

each visitor; it contains warm water to which they have given the name 'tea,' which is slightly red and highly medicinal." Two centuries later, it was the tax on this same beverage that sparked the American War of Independence in Boston Harbor.

Porcelain also made its way to the West. During the Ming dynasty, the fashion for "sacrifice red" enamel ended with the reign of Emperor Jia-jing. In the last twenty-five years of the sixteenth century, the Wan-li style produced the translucent and fragile porcelains decorated with the blue designs of the East India trading companies. They were worth their weight in gold.

A nation of one million people inhabited an empire that reached nearly every corner of the world, but there were repercussions. Already weakened by inflation brought on by its expanding empire, Portugal was further destabilized by a dynastic crisis with the death in Morocco of the young Sebastian I. In 1580, the crown passed to Philip II of Spain via the tangled network of relationships linking Portugal and Spain—two countries separated by fierce nationalism, yet united by many family alliances.

Philip was at war against the United Provinces, so the Lisbon warehouses were closed in 1594 to the "sea-beggars" who sent exotic products to the Netherlands. Their boats were confiscated and their Lutheran crews subjected to the Inquisition. The following year, a Dutch fleet set sail from Amsterdam, heading for the Indian Ocean. In 1619, Jakarta became Batavia. Overwhelmed, the Portuguese empire of the East Indies crumbled as quickly as it had been constructed. Yet it left indelible marks: an entrenched Catholic Church and a common language. For many years, even in Batavia, Portuguese was the language spoken in the offices of the East India trading companies.

Preceding double page: Arrival of a Portuguese argosy, or *nau,* in Nagasaki. Gouache on mulberry paper with gold leaf, affixed to a panel. Detail of a screen attributed to Kano Naizen. The series of "Namban byôbu" (the southern barbarian screens), made between 1590 and 1640, demonstrates the interest shown by painters of the Kano school in scenes of everyday life. The unexpected arrival of the Portuguese at Tanegashima, near Kyushi, in 1543, followed by their settlement in the port of Nagasaki, offered these Japanese artists an exotic subject. They created humorous renderings of the clothing, attitudes, and long noses of the foreigners.

D. Alfonso de Albuquerque (1462-1515). Anonymous portrait on wood, painted in Goa in the mid-sixteenth century. It was part of a series of portraits of the Indian governors, begun in 1547 on orders of D. Joáo de Castro and overseen by Gaspar Correira.

The Castle of Batavia.
Oil painting by
A. Beeckman, 1656.
The Dutch entered Jakarta
by force in 1612, and
on May 12, 1619 founded
Batavia, the heart of
the powerful Vereenigde
Oostindische Compagnie,
known as the VOC. It was
an industrial shipyard,
the port from which ships
in the Amsterdam fleets
were dispersed throughout
all of Indonesia, and the
central storehouse for
exotic cargo before it was
shipped to Europe.

Preceding double page:
Detail of the first map
of the New World, drawn
in 1500 near Cadix by
a Basque pilot, Juan de la
Cosa, owner and pilot of
the *Santa Maria.*

Opposite page: The retable
of *Our Lady of Navigators,*
painted by Alejo Fernandez
(1497) for the chapel of
the Casa de Contratación,
depicts the Virgin
protecting the ships and
men involved in the
conquest of the New World
by shielding them with
her mantle. Church
dignitaries, captains,
religious figures, and
seafarers hold the newly
converted Indians in the
shadows in check, in what
could be an allusion to a
narthex.

Right:
Portrait of Christopher
Columbus. Anonymous
miniature, sixteenth
century.

As we know, the discovery of America was one of the greatest misconceptions in the history of mankind. Columbus was not seeking to discover a New World, but rather a sea route to the East Indies that would be more direct than the one taken by the Portuguese. According to the prevailing view of the time, he was sailing toward Asia. India, heretofore situated on the right-hand side of the mappa mundi reserved for Lusitanian exploration, suddenly sprang up on the left-hand side of the map as well. The Christian monarchs saw themselves as the natural protectorates of primitive civilizations, and to clear up any confusion over territorial claims, Pope Alexander VI issued a decree in 1493 establishing a demarcation line through the mid-Atlantic, with Spain gaining possession of any unclaimed territories to the west of the line and Portugal to the east. The Portuguese gained possession of Brazil; Spain conquered the remainder of the New World until other rulers excluded from the partition soon began to make claims of their own.

Navigators in both the East and West had been relying on the sun to determine direction in the inhabitable part of the world—between Libya and the southern reaches of a burning desert and the northern reaches of the cold Hyperborean night—since the dawn of time. Aristotle and Greek geographers maintained that the Earth was round, and there were rough estimates of the actual size of the planet itself, although there was some confusion over the unit of measurement.

As one of the advanced minds of the time, Christopher Columbus developed accurate theories based on erroneous data. The world was believed to be smaller, and Eurasia much larger than it actually was, making his seemingly foolhardy idea feasible. According to the technical and intellectual theories at the time, a ship could cross the only ocean separating the Iberian peninsula from China and India by sailing due west. The problem resided in knowing whether it was actually possible to reach the other side of the world, and more acutely if it was possible to get back. Isabella of Castile appointed a commission of scholars in 1486 to evaluate the project submitted by a scatterbrained man with gray eyes. The foreigner, a skilled expert in maps, charts, and navigation, maintained that India could be reached by sailing due west.

The scholars met in the Dominican convent in Salamanca and delivered their verdict after four years of reflection and scientific and theological research: Columbus's theory was sheer nonsense. The committee noted that Saint Augustine had ruled out passage from one hemisphere to the next. Yet the Portuguese had crossed the equator a quarter of a century earlier and were moving about freely within the southern hemisphere.

Geocentrism bolstered the corollary notion of a motionless Earth at the center of the universe, with an above and a below. Hence, there was no reason to set out to confirm the actual geographical layout of the world, the image of which was determined by dogma inherent in the Bible. Maps of the world in two hemispheres, in an effort to depict a spherical world on a flat surface, lent support to the visual juxtaposition of east and west, one being on the right and the other on the left of the vellum.

Intellectual theories that fortunately proved accurate despite erroneous parameters lay behind the discovery of America, but chance was also involved. A watershed event, albeit a somewhat intangible factor in the history of mankind, was the fall of Granada on January 2, 1492 to the army of the Spanish monarchs. The event marked the end of nearly eight centuries of occupation by the Moors and four centuries of conquest. In the wake of the success in Granada, Spain began to reassess its policies concerning maritime exploration and turned to Columbus, despite the initial rejection of his theories by Isabella's scholars. He was recalled to the Spanish court, having departed to convince other kings of the merits of his obsession. The royal decree was signed on April 17, and America— or at least an inextricable string of islands that seemed somewhat remote from popular conceptions of India and Asia at the time—was discovered on the following October 12.

SAN SALVADOR

Columbus's log from his first voyage has not survived, although we have a good abstract of it, written in the 1530s by Bartolome de Las Casas, the first priest ordained in the New World, later named bishop, who denounced the atrocities committed against the Amerindians. Tension was mounting aboard Spanish ships heading due west from the Canary Islands, and the crewmembers were seized with fear. "Land!" had been shouted out night after night, yet nothing but clouds lay on the horizon. Still, a powerful odor of humus had been wafting through the air for three days, a sign that tropical vegetation was near. Flocks of birds and floating debris also provided signs of approaching land.

On the night of October 11, 1492, land was first sighted from aboard the *Pinta*—the swiftest of the fleet capering in the lead. The ships hove to and partially furled their sails, and refrains of *Salve Regina* were heard. On Thursday,

Right:
The ex-voto of Mataro. This votive model is the oldest ship model housed in maritime museums throughout the world. The hull of the Mataro dates from Columbus's time; he most probably saw the ship. It was built by a Catalan sailor or carpenter toward the mid-fifteenth-century, then offered to Saint-Simon of Mataro just a few kilometers from Barcelona. It's a "coconut," a medieval term for the round-shaped hull of a trade ship.

the Spaniards finally set foot on solid ground. It was not yet the continent, probably only Watling Island, one of the tiniest isles of the Bahaman nebula off the vast undiscovered barrier of the Americas stretching from the North to the South Pole. It was certainly not Kublai Khan's China or Marco Polo's Cathay.

Columbus was hailed by the same men who, days earlier, were ready to lynch the foreigner who had seemed to so carelessly toss their fate into the sea and whom great Spanish scholars had branded a madman.

"Here follow the precise words of the admiral from the log of his first voyage in discovering the Indies: 'As I saw that they were very friendly to us, and perceived that they could be much more easily converted to our holy faith by gentle means than by force, I presented them with some red caps, and strings of beads to wear upon the neck, and many other trifles of small value, wherewith they were much delighted.... I saw no beasts in the island, nor any sort of animals except parrots.'"

Columbus seemed not to understand how people so naked and poor could be living so near to the Great Khan's capital and to Cipango with its golden palace. He proposed an ingenious explanation for this nagging question. "I saw some with scars of wounds upon their bodies, and demanded by signs the origin of them; they answered me in the same way, that there came people from the other islands in the neighborhood who endeavored to make prisoners of them, and they defended themselves. I thought then, and still believe, that these were from the continent. It appears to me, that the people are ingenious, and would be good servants... If it please our Lord, I intend at my return to carry home six of them to Your Highnesses, that they may learn our language."

The admiral decided to set sail on October 14, heading "southwest in search of gold and precious stones," thus completing his mission. Things went smoothly. "When I have discovered the places rich in gold and spices, I will stop as long as required to take as much as possible. So I am setting out to look for them... I will pass by the small islands en route to the larger ones, and based on whether I find gold or spices, I will decide how best to proceed. But I am ever determined to

Goldsmiths found great inspiration in the rounded voluminous shapes of Renaissance cargo vessels. The "Charles V treasure-ship" is one of the masterpieces produced by the Augsburg workshops in the sixteenth and seventeenth centuries. Works included goblets, table centerpieces, and inkwells shaped like ships. Master glassmakers from Murano, Nuremberg, and Baccarat also produced these types of objects. Details from the "Charles V treasure-ship," an automated clock dating from circa 1580 and attributed to German clocksmith Hans Schlottheim.

A Tapuya native. The island of Maranhào (Sào Luis), north of Brazil, was frequented by the Dieppois in the late-sixteenth century. Daniel de La Ravardière and the brothers François and Isaac de Razilly thought of establishing Saint-Louis here, the capital of a hypothetical France settlement in the western hemisphere. They lived here for four years before the Portuguese forced them to move on. Itinerant colonists provided mediation during disputes between the Tabajare, Tupinamba, and Tapuya Indians. Illustration from Zacharias Wagner's travel log, circa 1634.

Presently they descried people, naked, and the admiral landed in the boat, which was armed, along with Martin Alonso Pinzon, and Vincente Yañez his brother, captain of the *Niña*. The admiral bore the royal standard, and the two captains each a banner of the Green Cross, which all the ships had carried; this contained the initials of the names of the King and Queen each side of the cross, and a crown over each letter. The natives called their island Guanahani. Columbus named it San Salvador and took possession of the island. Arrived on shore, they saw trees very green, many streams of water, and diverse sorts of fruits. The admiral called upon the two captains, and the rest of the crew who landed, as also to Rodrigo de Escovedo notary of the fleet, and Rodrigo Sanchez, of Segovia, to bear witness that he before all others took possession (as in fact he did) of that island for the king and queen his sovereigns, making the requisite declarations, which are more at large set down here in writing. Numbers of the people of the island straightway collected together.

Christopher Columbus. Friday, October 12, 1492.
Copy by Bartolome de Las Casas of the original logbook, which has since disappeared.

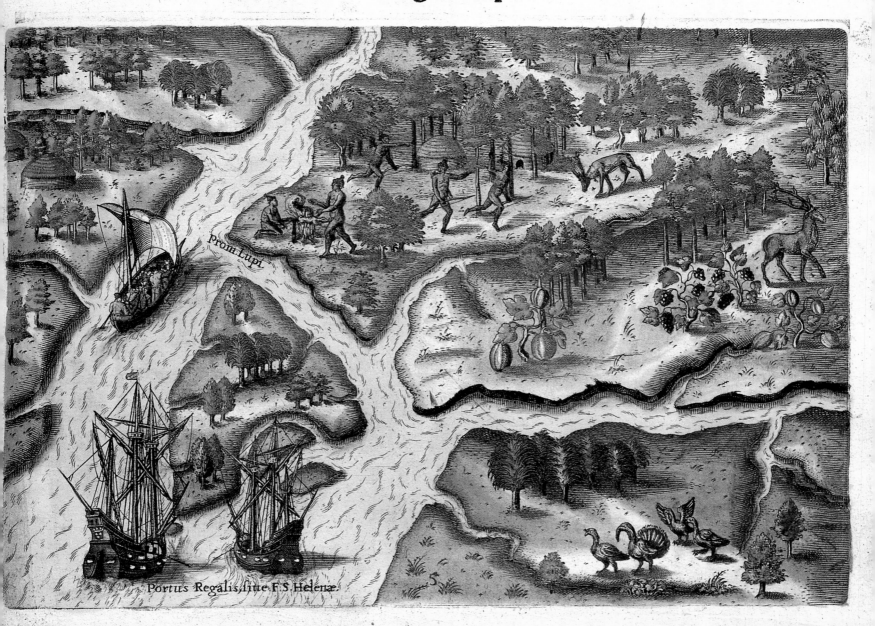

Prom. Lupi.

Portus Regalis, sive F. S. Helenæ.

TER solitum persequentes, amnem invenerunt. quem Conspectu bellum nuncuparunt: dein tria aut quatuor miliaria ulterius emensi cum essent, ipsis significatum, non procul inde abesse latum aliud flumen magnitudine & amœnitate reliqua superans: quò progressi, ob ejus amœnitatem & amplitudinem Regalem portum appellarunt. Istic subductis velis, anchoras ad decem orgyias jecerunt: descensione à Præfecto & militibus in continentem facta, amœnissimum esse locum compererunt: nam quercubus, cedris, & alijs arborum generibus consitus erat. Per quas incedentes, Indicos pavones, sive Galli-pavos prætervolantes, & cervos per syluam errantes conspiciebant. Hujus fluminis ostium latum est tribus Gallicis leucis sive miliaribus, & in duo cornua dividitur; quorum alterum ad Occidentem vergit, alterum ad Septentrionem, idque (secundum quorundam opinionem) interiora regionis penetrans, ad flumen Iordanem tendit: alterum in mare relabitur, ut ab inquilinis observatum est. Patent hæc bina cornua magnis duobus miliaribus in latitudinem, & in eorum medio insula est, cujus cuspis fluminis ostium spectat. Paulo post navi denuo conscensa, cornu ad Occidentem se convertens ingressi sunt, ut ejus commoditates observarent: & emensis circiter duodecim miliaribus, Indorum catervam conspexerunt, qui scaphis animadversis illico, fugæ se mandarunt, relicto quem assabant lupi cervarij catulo: cujus rei causa eum locum Lupi promontorium appellarunt. Ulterius navigantes, in aliam fluminis diuisionem inciderunt, ab Oriente labentem, per quam Præfectus, relicto majore alveo, navigare statuit.

Left:
The French Arrive in Port Royal (Florida). French attempts to settle in America in the mid-sixteenth-century were rejected by Iberian monarchs refusing to share the newly claimed territories. Jean Ribault and René de Laudonnière's men and women were captured in 1565, cruelly tortured, and massacred on Philip II's orders, on the grounds of being enemies of Spain and of being Lutherans. Hand-painted engraving by Théodore de Bry after Jacques Lemoyne de Morgues. Ribault and Laudonnière's voyage to Florida, (1562-1565). *Grands Voyages,* 1591.

Background image: Caribbean Indians. This series of four illustrations reflects the exoticism and paradoxes of the New World: the skill of the paddlers whose light *canoas* impressed Columbus; men geared up for hunting and fishing; the gay frolicking of the natives; and the horror of eating human flesh, which instilled deep-seated fears of good Indians, the *Caribas* or *Canibas,* which were the origin of the terms Caribbean and cannibalism. *Géographie du Monde* by Artus Fonnant, 1633.

reach terra firma and in the city of Quinsay deliver the letters of Your Highnesses to the Great Khan." He was referring to what is today Hangzhou, the capital of the Song Dynasty in the south, which Marco Polo had visited and described in *The Description of the World,* this Venice of the east: "The so-called city of Quinsasy is so vast that it has some one hundred miles around it. There are twelve thousand stone bridges that are so high that a huge ship could pass underneath. And it should come as no surprise that the city has so many bridges, for I tell you the city lies in water and is surrounded by water... The ocean-sea is twenty-five miles from the city. The port is called Ganfu. There are many great ships coming and going to India and other exotic lands, carrying back and forth merchandise of all sorts, on which the city has built its fortune."

According to his own theories, as well as those of Toscanelli, or according to the globe which Martin Behaim designed in 1492 for the city of Nuremberg, Columbus could legitimately claim to have been within proximity of the capital of the Great Khan.

The flotilla continued from island to island, in search of a land the natives called Colba, or Cuba, "which I believe to be Cipango according to what the natives have told me about its splendor and riches... The island of Cuba is rich in spices and gold, frequented by the great merchant ships... I am certain it is the island of Cipango, whose wonders are legendary, which I have seen on the globes

and the maps of the world and which is located somewhere in these latitudes."
They arrived in Cuba on October 28. "The admiral said he had never seen a land
so beautiful. Just by the bank were green and lush trees, so different from ours
and each with its own flowers and fruit. Many different types of birds were seen,
each with a soft mellow song. Even better, the natives claimed there were pearls
and gold mines on the island. The admiral espied a likely spot where the former

*How the Portuguese Sent a
Second Vessel to Locate Me.*
Hans Staden, the author of
the original drawing from
which these two engravings
were inspired, had been
captured and made prisoner
by the Tupinamba. He was

both a hostage and
potential food stock for
cannibals who grilled their
victims on a *barbacoa*.
Hand-painted engraving by
Théodore de Bry. *Grands
Voyages,* 1592.

might be found as well, as the oyster shells that indicated their presence. The
investigation took shape and ambassadors were sent to make contact with the
Khan. As a result of some linguistic misunderstandings, the gold which the
natives referred to as *nuçay* appeared now to come from Bohio or from Bavèque
in the southwest of the island. The ships set anchor beside the beach.

All during their explorations, the Spanish were distracted by many unfamiliar
things that were to enrich their store of unexpected discoveries. Bedding, for

"When we were four hundred miles away from the Barbary Coast, we saw around the vessel a school of fish which we caught using hooks. (...) We also saw fish as large as herrings,

example, was suspended in cabins by the natives on the island of Fernandina. "Their beds, covers, and wall hangings were like cotton nets." Other explorers, Pêro Vaz de Caminha, secretary to Pedro Alvares Cabral, and Amerigo Vespucci, also described these hammocks a few years later, which were used all along the coast of Brazil and from Central America to the Gulf of Mexico. Sailors all over the world would eventually adopt the hammock. Columbus noted the quality of

with wings like those of bats on either side: the great men stalked them as prey."
Hand-painted engraving by Théodore de Bry. *Grands Voyages*, 1592.

their skiffs, the *canoas,* "long boats, carved from a single tree trunk and all of a piece. They row them with a sort of baker's paddle and they move quite wonderfully through the water."

In addition to the cottonweed, mastic trees, and a few plants such as manioc, corn, and beans, Columbus noticed on October 15, among the humble belongings of the occupant of a pirogue intercepted between the islands of Santa Maria and Fernandina, "a few dried leaves which were probably considered of great value by them, as they had already brought me some as a present in San Salvador." On November 6, two men dispatched to find gum trees along the northern coast of Cuba also noticed "many people heading toward their village, both men and women, carrying half-burned leaves for smoking, as was their custom."

Las Casas provided the first description, in his *History of the Indies,* of Havana cigars—"dried herbs wrapped in a certain leaf that was also dried and shaped like the paper firecrackers that boys make during Pentecost. They light one end, then suck or draw on or inhale the smoke inwards which makes their skin go numb and they nearly become inebriated. They claim that they don't feel tired. They named the firecrackers, or whatever they were called, tobacco. I knew some Spanish people on the island of Hispaniola who regularly used it, and after I upbraided them and emphasized that this was a vice, retorted that they were unable to stop using it. I can't imagine what kind of flavor or taste they were drawn to with it." Thus from the moment tobacco was discovered, the problem of giving up smoking was an issue.

THE FORT AT NATIVITY

"Today I placed the ship back into the waters and I am in great haste to leave Thursday, in the name of the Lord, for the southeast to seek gold and spices, and new land." But due to the poor weather, the Spanish did not actually set sail until November 12. They reached what Columbus thought was Bohio and named Hispaniola on December 6. This was Haiti-Dominican Republic. "All the trees are green and full of fruit, and the plants are in flower and very tall. The roads are wide and good, and the breezes are like those in Castile in the month of April. The nightingales and other small birds sing as they do in Spain in the same month, and it is the greatest pleasure in the world. Small birds sing sweetly during the night, and one can hear many crickets and frogs. The fish are the same as in Spain. There are many mastic trees, aloe, and cottonwood. No gold has been found, but this is not surprising since we have been here such a short time..."

On the night of December 25, the Spanish were jolted back to reality when the *Santa Maria* ran aground in Manzanillo Bay. "Our Lord wished that, at the twelfth hour of the night, having seen the admiral retire to his quarters to get some rest, and seen that it was dead calm and the sea was as smooth as water in a saucer, everyone retire to sleep. The helm was left in the hands of this boy; and the current swept the ship into one of the sandbanks. The waters were crashing so loudly against it that it could be heard from afar, and although it was night, could be seen. The ship came so slowly up against the bank that it was barely noticed. The young man, who sensed that the rudder was no longer

Pacoba and *Zaranga.* These were the names of the common banana and orange, according to the Maranhào of Brazil. Various discoveries introduced a whole range of exotic flora and fauna to Europe. Many of the fruits and vegetables are commonly found today. Watercolors from Zacharias Wagner's travel log, circa 1634.

53

Pacoba

51. Laranga.

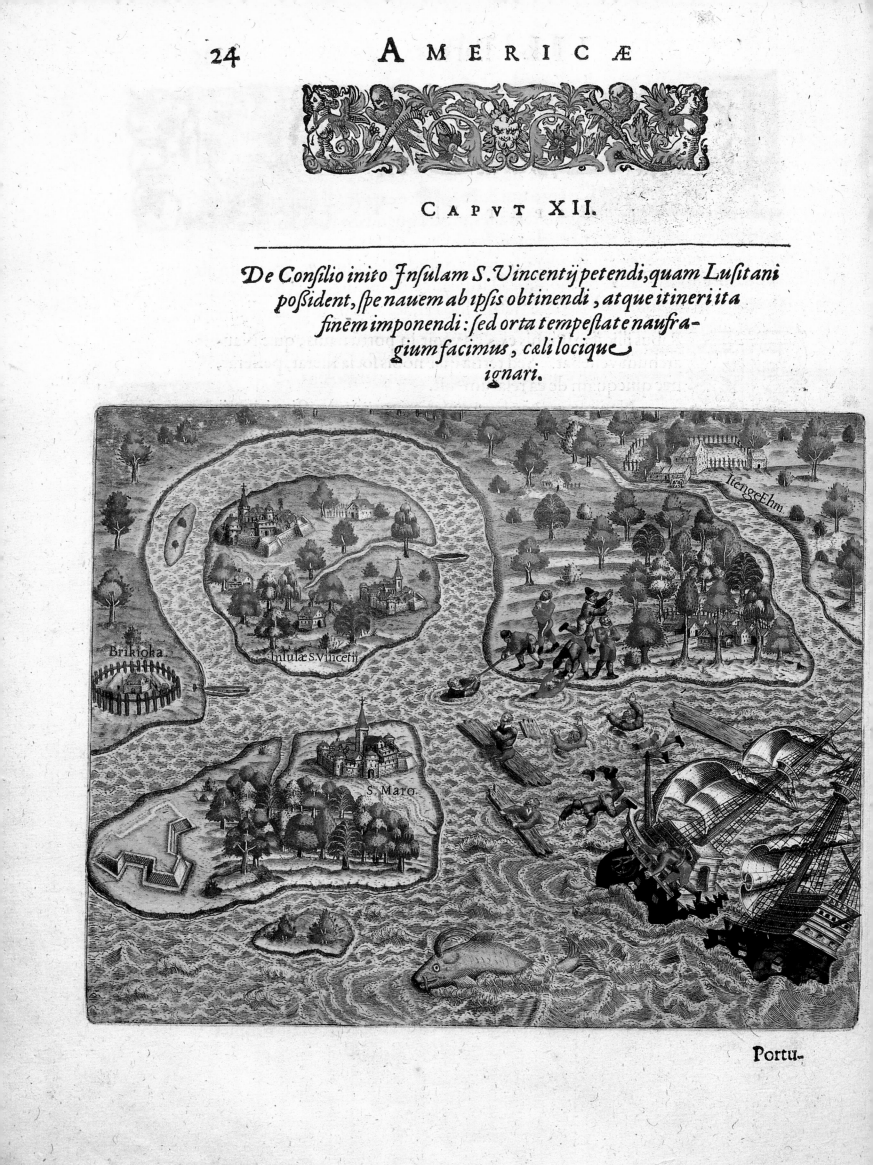

CAPVT XII.

De Consilio inito Jnsulam S. Vincentij petendi, quam Lusitani possident, spe nauem ab ipsis obtinendi, atque itineri ita finem imponendi: sed orta tempestate naufragium facimus, cæli locique ignari.

Portu-

In which we speak of the decision taken to go to the island of Saint Vincent, a Portuguese possession; of the way to obtain a ship, and how it was shipwrecked during a storm.
Hand-painted engraving by Théodore de Bry after a wood engraving and Hans Staden's narrative. *Grands Voyages,* 1592.

"Mulatto smoking." Columbus was the first to describe tobacco and the way in which the inhabitants of Cuba smoked. The Spanish later adopted the custom and were "no longer able to refrain from using it," which surprised Bartolome de Las Casas. Drawing by Charles Plumier, 1688.

under his control and could hear the sound of the surf, began to shout. The admiral heard him and came out so quickly that no one else had time to notice that they had run aground."

The description of the chaos that reigned reveals that all rescue attempts failed. The ship fell against its side as the tide went out, its seams burst, and the vessel was lost. The admiral's confused and contradictory account reveals his embarrassment in explaining such a serious and inexcusable accident. During the course of his account, he reiterated that it was officially forbidden to entrust the helm to a ship's boy and he himself had pointed out the bay the evening before. One factor that may have entered into the equation is that the crew and officers of a ship baptized *Santa Maria,* adventuring to the far ends of the world, most likely celebrated Christmas with great fanfare.

The expedition turned sour. Martin Alonso Pinzon, who commanded the *Pinta,* separated from the fleet to look for gold for himself. All that remained for the admiral was the *Niña,* commanded by Vicente Pinzon, which was incapable of taking onboard those shipwrecked on Hispaniola.

Columbus showed great composure in redressing the situation. "He recognized that Our Lord had caused the ship to run aground so that it would remain there. And at that very moment, he says, so many things were at hand that in sooth it was no longer a disaster but a stroke of luck. It is indeed certain that if I had not run aground, I would have set out for the open seas without dropping anchor in this site ensconced in a large bay with perhaps two or three shoals. I would not have left people here on this voyage and even if I had wanted to, I would have been unable to supply them with vital supplies—enough munitions, food supplies, equipment, and rigging for shelter... Thus began preparations: timber to build the fortress; supplies of bread and wine to last over a year; seeds to sow; the launch of the ship with a caulker, carpenter, and bombardier, a cooper and many other men who avidly desired, to serve Your Majesty and to please me, to know where the mine was from which gold was to be extracted."

Unfortunately, the *canoas* dispatched one last time in the area found no gold, although they did return with a plant resembling rhubarb—"to show it to the Kings." As a precautionary measure when it came time to leave, the Indian chief Guacanagari was given an impressive show of artillery. The Spanish understood that the Indian chief "had commanded a statue of pure gold as big as the admiral himself" be built, but that it was not yet ready.

The Nativity Fort was the first European settlement in America. It was placed under the guard of thirty-nine men on January 4. They were all seamen and were commanded by three officers. Two days later, Columbus found the *Pinta.* The two caravels set off "directly for Spain" at daybreak on January 16, 1493. The two vessels were separated during a storm after a stopover in the Azores, and the *Niña* and the admiral accidentally ended up offshore from Lisbon. Ironically, it was John II of Portugal who first heard the account of the voyage and the discoveries.

On March 15, the welcome at Palos was worthy of the great event. The admiral and his companions, recounted Las Casas, "were led throughout the city in a great procession and it was a gala occasion. Great thanks was rendered to God for having allowed such a remarkable exploit and glorious feat to take place." The procession crossed Spain in four weeks, for the court was located in Barcelona. Sailors, soldiers, and the seven Indians brought back as proof of the exploit, preceded the admiral's horses and those of his sons, of the pilots, and the principal figures participating in the expedition. The spectators were treated to a splendidly exotic gala: weapons, Indian crafts, gold ornaments spread out widely to make up for the slenderness of the booty, necklaces made of seashells and feathers, cigars smoked with great pomp, tropical plants, and "some forty parrots, some green, others yellow, resembling the parrots commonly found in India, with vermilion rings around their necks." The rulers intoned the *Te Deum* on bended knee and invited the admiral to sit amongst them.

Each page of Columbus's travel log is filled with passages about gold. He gives accurate information indicating the location of the lodes, supplies evidence given to him by the inhabitants, and provides one pretext after another as to why they didn't bring any gold back. After christening a "River of Gold" on the northern coast of Hispaniola, "the admiral added with great flourish that he did not wish to take this sand so heavy with gold since Their Highnesses already had so much of it just outside their doorstep of their city of Nativity."

He addressed the famous letter announcing his discoveries to Luis de Santangel, the tax farmer who had pleaded with the Catholic monarchs to back Columbus's expedition. Indeed, Queen Isabella and King Ferdinand would first hear of the successful undertaking from the lips of Santangel. The letter added another touch of color to an already vivid picture. Hispaniola was described in superlative terms: "This island, as the others are, is supremely fertile, although perhaps even more slightly so. There are many ports along the sea coast which pale in comparison to the ones of Christianity that I have seen, and so many rivers that it is a sheer marvel to behold... Inland lie many mines and countless inhabitants. Hispaniola is a virtual splendor: the sierras and mountains, plains and valleys, land that is so beautiful and so rich, excellent for planting and sowing, for raising livestock of all sorts, for building towns and villages. One must behold the sight in order to believe the existence of the seaports and many rivers that are vast, with clean pure waters, many of which contain gold... On Hispaniola there are many spices, great gold mines, and other metals... By the signs they made, I think they thought that we came from Heaven. They were the first to announce this everywhere I went, and others went running from house to

ENOR por que se que aureis plazer dela grano vitoria que nuestro señor me ha dado en mi viaie vos escriuo esta por la ql sabreys como en xxxiii dias pase A las indias cō la armada q los illustrissimos Rey e Reyna ñros señores me dieron dōde yo falle muy muchas Islas pobladas cō gente sin numero: y dellas todas he tomado posesion por sus altezas con pregon y vādera rreal estendida y non me fue cōtradicho Ala primera q yo falle puse nōbre sant saluador a comemoraciō desu alta mage stat el qual marauillosamēte todo esto andado los idios la llamā guanahani Ala segūda puse nōbre la isla de santa maria de concepciō ala tercera ferrandina ala quarta la isla bella ala quita la Isla Iuana e asi a cada vna nōbre nueuo Quando yo llegue ala Iuana seg ui io la costa della al pōniente yla falle tan grāde q pense que seria tierra firme la prouicia de catayo y como no falle asi villas y luguares ēla costa dela mar saluo pequeñas poblaciones con la gente delas quales no podia hauer fabla por q: luego fuyan todos: andaua yo a de lante por el dicho camino pēsādo deno errar grādes Ciudades o villas y al cabo de muchas leguas visto q no hauia inouaciō i que la costa me leuaua al setētriō de adōde mi voluntad era cōtraria por q el yuierno era ya ēcarnado yo tenia proposito de hazer del al austro y tan biē el viēto medio adelāte determine deno aguardar otro tiēpo y bolui atras fasta vn señalado puer to de adōde ēbie dos hōbres por la tierra para saber si hauia Rey o grādes Ciudades ādoui erō tres iornadas y hallarō iñitas poblaciōes pequeñas i gēte si numero mas no cosa de reg imiēto por lo qual se boluierō yo entēdia harto de otros idios q ia tenia tomados como cōti nuamēte esta tierra era Isla e asi segui la costa della al oriēte ciento i siete leguas fasta dōde fa zia fin del qual cabo vi otra Isla al oriēte disticta de esta diez o ocho leguas ala qual luego puse nombre la spañola y fui alli y segui la parte del setentriō asi como dela iuana al oriēte. clxxviii grādes leguas por linia recta del oriēte asi como dela iuana la qual y todas las otras sō fortissimas en demasiado grado y esta enestremo en ella ay muchos puertos enla costa dela mar si cōparaciō de otros q yo sepa en cristianos y fartos rrios y buenos y grādes q es mara villa las tierras della sō altas y ē ella muy muchas sierras y mōtañas altissimas si cōparaciō de la isla de cētre frei todas fermosissimas de mil fechuras y todas ādabiles y llenas de arboles de mil maneras i altas i parecen q llegā al cielo i tēgo por dicho q iamas pierdē la foia segun lo puede cōprehēder q los vi tā verdes i tā hermosos como sō por mayo en spaña i dellos estauā flor ridos dellos cō fruto i dellos en otro termino segū es su calidad i cātaua el ruiseñor i otros pa xaricos de mil maneras en el mes de nouiembre por alli dōde io ādaua ay palmas de seis o de ocho maneras q es admiracion verlas por la difformidad fermosa dellas mas asicomo los o otros arboles y frutos e ieruas en ella ay pinares amarauilla e ay cāpiñas gradissimas e ay mi el i de muchas maneras de aues y frutas muy diuersas enlas tierras ay muchas minas de me tales e ay gēte estimabile numero La spañola es marauilla las sierras y las mōtañas y las uegas illas campiñas y las tierras tan fermosas y gruesas para plātar y sēbrar pacriar ganados de to das suertes para hedificios de villas e lugares los puertos dela mar aqui no hauria crehēcia sin vista y delos rios muchos y grandes y buenas aguas los mas delos quales trahē oro ē los arbo les y frutos e ieruas ay grandes differēcias de aquel las dela iuana en esta ay muchas spece rias y grandes minas de oro y de otros metales. La gente desta isla e de todas las otras q he fallado y hauido ni aya hauido noticia andan todos desnudos hōbres y mugeres asi como sus madres los parē haun que algunas mugeres se cobiā vn solo lugar cō vna foia de yer ua: o vna cosa de algodō q para ello fazen ellos no tienē fierro ni azero ni armas ni sō para ello no por que no sea gente bien dispuesta y de fermosa estatura saluo que sō muy te amarauilla no tienē otras armas saluo las armas delas cañas quando dl con la siuiēte o la qual ponen al cabo vn palillo agudo eno osan vsar de aqllas que mi vezes me ēbiar a enuiar a hora dos o tres hombres a alguna villa para hauer fabla. salier

Left:
Huehueteotl, god of fire and the mother and father of all gods. Columbus's futile search for a passage to East Indies, during the three subsequent journeys following his maiden voyage, nearly led to the discovery of Mexican and Peruvian civilizations between Guyana and the Yucatan. Much later, Hernán Cortés marched on Tenochtitlán (Mexico) on August 16, 1519. Columbus died unknown in Valladolid on May 20, 1506, eighteen months after his protectress Isabella of Castile. The breadth and scope of his discovery had not yet been realized. Terra cotta, Veracruz, Mexico, 600-800.

Right:
Zapoteca anthropomorphic funerary urn,
450-650.
Oaxaca region, Mexico.

house and to neighboring villages, shouting: 'Come behold the people from Heaven!' All of them, men and women, as soon as they were reassured as to what we really were, flocked around us in one massive crowd, and everyone brought something to eat or to drink, which they offered with the greatest pleasure... It was here in Hispaniola, in the most suitable place, the closest to the gold mines and the best for all circulation, in terms of both our terra ferma and that of the Great Khan, there where a source of great commerce and profit, that I took possession of a great city that I named the city of Nativity. And here I had a great wall and fortress built which, by now, must be complete... On another island, which, I am told, is even larger than Hispaniola, there is so much gold that it cannot be counted, and the Indians whom I bring with me will be able to testify to this, as to everything else I have described. In conclusion, and to not speak only of what transpired during this voyage, which was only a day's run, Their Highnesses can rest assured that I will give them gold, as much as they need, and so slight the assistance they will have to grant me; as much spices and cotton as they request right now, as much mastic gum as they wish us to carry, ... and aloe plants as well, as much as they ask us to carry, and slaves whom we will make idolators. I believe I have also found rhubarb and cinnamon, and I will find thousands of other valuable items which the people whom I have left there will have discovered."

The astounding journey Columbus had experienced with his companions measured up to the marvels expected from explorers. The admiral may have been tempted to exaggerate the outcome of the expedition, yet what he saw and shared with his companions was not unusual. Numerous travel logs dating from this period are riddled with legends and superstitions. To his countrymen, the pallisaded village of huts built in a week using timber salvaged from the *Santa Maria* could easily have been the powerful fortress erected on the other side of the world in the rich city of Nativity.

Two weeks after his return to Spain, even before even leaving Palos for the court, Columbus received orders to prepare as quickly as possible for a new expedition. "It will please God that, for what you have already accomplished, you will receive many favors which, in sooth, will be granted to you in response to your services and work, and because we wish that with the assistance of God, what you have begun shall be pursued and carried further, and we desire your presence at the earliest possible time to serve us. Make as great haste as is possible, so that we can provide all that is required, and because, as you see, summer has already begun and we must not delay your returning to the land which you have discovered." The fitting out took six months and, on September 25, a fleet of seventeen ships set out from Cadix for the Indies with one thousand five hundred men, amid the excitement and fever of a gold rush.

The Lesser Antilles were discovered during the second voyage. The islands were named Dominica, which appeared on the horizon on Sunday; Marie-Galante, after the flagship; Los Santos, and Désirade. Guadeloupe was named after the blessing made to Santa Maria de la Guadalupe during a violent storm on the journey back, and after the royal monastery which the Portuguese crew also invoked. In Basse Terre, the Spanish found indications of cannibalism, evidence of the presence of the fearsome Caniba or Cariba Indians, whom they had heard about during the first journey. Most islands of the Lesser Antilles were named as far north as Puerto Rico. The fleet sighted Hispaniola on November 22 and, five days later, in the middle of the night, they reached the fort at Nativity. The Spanish were calm. "Neither the king nor his subjects knew what weapons are. They go about naked, as I had mentioned, and are the most cowardly people in the world. Thus the few men I left there would be sufficient to ransack the entire country, and if they know how to go about it, the island presents absolutely no danger to them."

Diego Alvarez Chanca, the ship's doctor, recounts the return to Hispaniola in his travel log: "We anchored at the above mentioned place, and the admiral immediately ordered that two mortars be shot to see if the Christians whom he had left with the aforementioned Guacanari answered, for they had mortars as well. But we had no response and did not see the faintest fire or indication of dwelling in this place. Everyone felt a great affliction and such suspicion that was warranted in such a situation."

"The next day, the admiral came aground accompanied by a few of our men and we headed toward what should have been the town. We found that it had been burned to the ground, and there were articles of clothing that belonged to the Christians scattered about on the grass." It was learned later that, as soon as the caravels had departed, the Spanish from the Nativity fort had started fighting one another with knives. They harassed the natives to seize what little gold they had, kidnapping their wives and daughters. They became hated, which surprised them, given their superior strength and the simplicity and passive nature of the natives—"loving people free of greed." An Indian chief organized the massacre of the Christians.

Left:
A *Duho*, a Haitian Taïno carved effigy seat. In November 1492 in Cuba, Rodrigo de Jerez and Luis de Torres, dispatched by Columbus on a reconnaissance mission, were solemnly seated on "seats made of solid wood, sculpted in strange animal forms, with very short legs and tails curving upwards forming a backrest. The heads were enormous and the eyes studded with gold." (The memoirs of Fernand Columbus.) Pre-Columbian art of the Antilles. (Taïno culture, Haiti.) This effigy seat in gaiac wood is said to have been brought back to Europe by Columbus.

Bottom left:
Tapuya woman. The author chose this caricatural depiction of a Tapuya woman heading home from the market to convey fears of the cruel customs of the natives of the island of Maranhào in Brazil. Illustration from Zacharias Wagner's travel log, circa 1634.

Right:
Oppidum Pomeiooc. This palisaded village is excerpted from *Admiranda Narratio*, Richard Greinville's account of a journey to Virginia by the English in 1585. Hand-painted engraving by Théodore de Bry. *Grands Voyages*, 1591.

ISABELA

The admiral founded a colony in the New World, Isabela, some one hundred kilometers east of the ransacked fort. Situated on an elevated point by the seaside, between a river and a forest, Isabela was protected by natural escarpments and a low stone walls. There were persistent outbreaks of fever, accompanied by doubts about finding vast amounts of gold. Yet there was enthusiasm, fueled by occasional discoveries. "The one that went to Cibao found gold in so many different places that no man dared say just how much. They found gold in over fifty rivers and streams, as well as along riverbanks. As a result, it was said that gold could be found throughout the entire province, wherever people looked. They took samples in various places, in the sand of riverbeds and other sources of water, as well as samples of gold found on the ground. They believe that digging into the ground the way we do is the way to unearth larger pieces of gold, for the Indians do not dig and do not have adequate tools for digging deep. The group that went to Niti also brought back the news that there is a great deal of gold in three or four locations; they too brought back samples. Therefore, with great certitude, the Kings our Lords can now consider themselves the most prosperous and wealthiest monarchs in existence, for nothing like it has been seen anywhere else in the world. When the ships make the next trip back, they most certainly will be able to carry back such vast quantities of gold that it will dazzle anyone who knows."

The report to the Catholic Kings that Columbus gave to the captain of the *Marie-Galante,* Antonio de Torres, in late January 1494, was even more triumphant. "We found so many rivers filled with gold that those who saw them could pluck the gold from the river with their hands, as a sample, and returned so overjoyed and spoke about such abundance that I am troubled to say this and write this to Their Highnesses." This discovery was, however, speculative. The admiral pointed out his shortcomings in manpower and in mules for transporting goods. He requested additional material and men.

During the month of June 1494, Fernando Perez de Luna, a notary to Isabella, recorded the following statements by Columbus: "Thus I publicly summoned, on the caravel *Niña,* the master and his company, people whose names and city of residence I will list below. Likewise for the two other aforementioned caravels, I summoned the masters and their company, and a similar declaration before witnesses mentioned below. I summoned them as the aforesaid lord admiral had requested me to, under penalty of paying ten thousand *maravedi* for whoever would claim the opposite of what until now he has said, and each time that this occurs; under penalty of having one's tongue cut out, for cabin boys and the like, that in a similar case they shall receive one hundred blows of the *garcette* and their tongues be cut out. All were thus summoned, on all three ships, each for his

Background image: Columbus's signature on a manuscript from the monastery of Rábida near Palos. The explorer saw evidence of his having been chosen by God in the derivation of his name, Cristoforo, from *Christo ferens,* or Christ's messenger.

Pre-Columbian pendants from Panama. Spanish conquerors were very disappointed to discover that the Indians' jewels and precious objects frequently were not made of pure gold. They were often made of *tumbaga,* a mixture of gold and copper, which was quite beautiful in appearance but was a humble material and produced very little precious metal when cast.

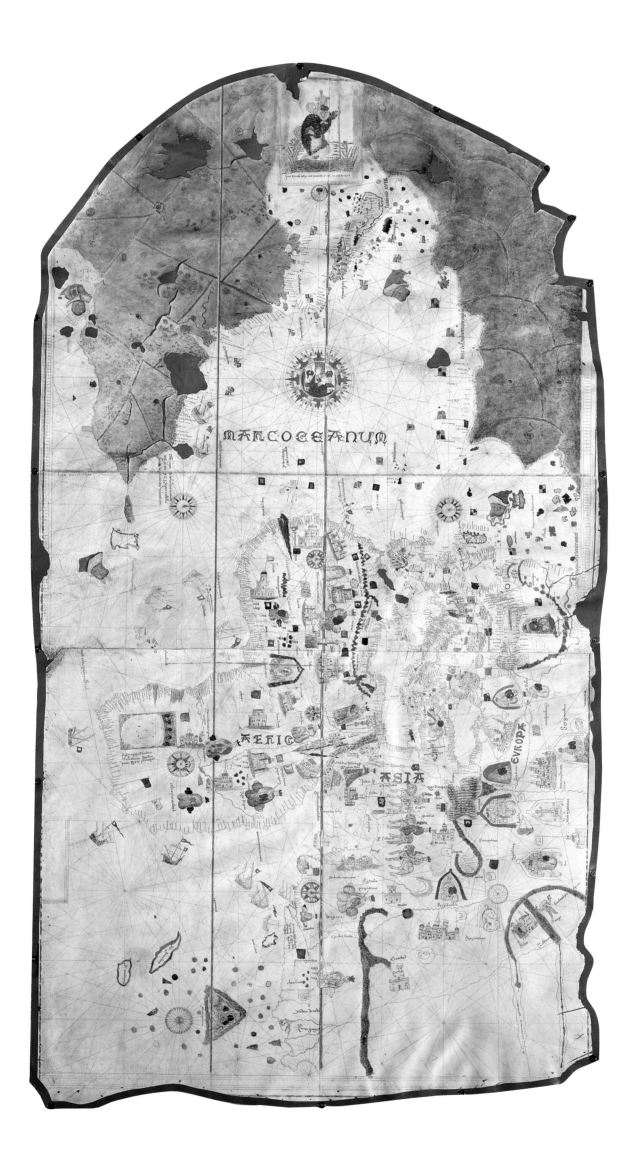

Left:
The first map of the
New World. It was drawn
in 1500 near Cadix by
a Basque navigator, Juan
de la Cosa, master and
commander of the *Santa
Maria.* The Mappa Mundi
is displayed here with
the west on top. A huge
landmass lies on the other
side of the Atlantic,
named *Mare Oceanum*
at the time. The barrier
lying to the west does not
yet try to reconcile
Columbus's discovery and
Asia according to Ptolemy.
The mapmaker masked
the theoretical passage
to India by an image
of Saint Christopher,
undoubtedly an allusion
to Christopher Columbus.

Columbus's signature on a
manuscript from the
monastery of Rábida.
There are several
hypotheses as to the
initials, one being *Sanctus,
Sanctus, Sanctus, Xhristus,
Maria, Yosephus,* or
*Xhristobal, Almirante
Mayor Yndias Sub Scripsi*
(the undersigned).

own account. With great diligence, the pilots, masters, and seamen studied their maps of the sea, reflected, and stated the following: Francisco Niño de Moguer, pilot of the caravel *Niña,* states that, by the oath he has taken, he has never heard of nor seen the island which is said to be three hundred thirty-five leagues along one coast, from west to east—all of the island not having yet been covered. And he now sees that the Earth turns south-southwest and southwest and west, and certainly there is no doubt that this is terra firma. In contrast, he affirmed and maintained that it was terra firma, not an island, and that before many leagues, sailing along the aforesaid coast, one would find a land inhabited by people who were refined and worldly. Similar statements were made by Alonso Medel de Palos, master of the *Niña,* by Juan de la Cosa, of the port of Santa Maria, master mapmaker of the *Niña,* and by all other sailors, cabin boys, and other figures aboard the aforesaid caravel and who agreed on things of the sea. The same oath was taken by the crew and passengers of the caravel *San Juan* and the caravel *Cardera,* the witnesses of the oath signing last."

In this way, Columbus's companions unanimously declared that Cuba was China. They were barely a few miles from Cape San Antonio, the extreme northern tip of the island, which would have set them straight. In the bad weather that hampered their voyage, the three caravels were forced to battle their way through shallows off the southern coast of Cuba. The admiral came up with this solution to simplify matters and expedite things.

Juan de la Cosa, an experienced pilot and expert on the Antilles sea, must have been skeptical, as he hesitated little in reneging on his oath, when he accurately drew Cuba seven years later, in 1501, on the earliest sea map depicting the New World. This historic mappa mundi sketched out a vast landmass that was uniformly dark in the western section of the Atlantic, which was still called *Mare Oceanum,* according to ancient tradition of the ocean periphery. It stands out clearly from the light outline of the shores of Europe and western Africa, a dark,

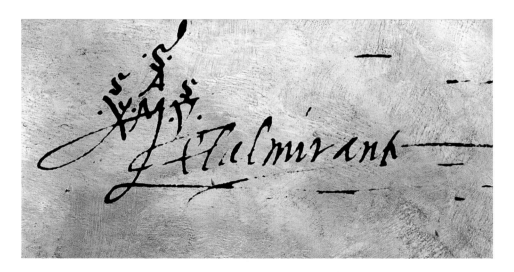

mysterious region. At the site of the isthmus of Panama, a vignette depicting Saint Christopher conveniently masks the spot where a passage to the west should logically exist. Columbus looked for it in vain, nearly at the same time as La Cosa was drawing out his map.

PARADISE ON EARTH

In 1498, the war against France for territory in Italy and the strategic marriage of the Infante Dona Juana ("La Loca") with Philip I of Holland were much more important issues for Spain's future than the muddled exploration of the Indies. The excitement over ill-advised Indians and a few fragments of gold had died down. Columbus was a source of great jealousy and his legitimacy was thrown into question. Doubts over the latter, however, were dispelled by his friendship with Queen Isabella, despite the open hostility of King Ferdinand. Once again, Columbus had triumphed over his enemies, albeit only for a short period of time.

Vasco da Gama had been in Calicut for ten days when the admiral's third fleet set sail. The route to India had just been opened, although this was not yet known in Europe. Columbus's fleet split into two squadrons: three ships sailed directly for Hispaniola with supplies for the colonists there; but the other three, commanded by Columbus himself, were on a mission of exploration, attempting to find any lands south of the known islands in the West Indies. On July 31, just as Columbus was about to renounce his mission and head north under a leaden sun, the look-out sighted land. Because the island had three hills, Columbus named it Trinidad, after the Holy Trinity. The fleet obtained water on the south coast of Trinidad, and in the process sighted the coast of South America, the first Europeans to see that continent. Columbus was worried about the heavy seas and strong currents, but he was particularly concerned about the presence of fresh water in the sea. That fresh water had reached so far offshore indicated that a very powerful river flowed into the Gulf of Paria. He was in fact offshore from the mouth of the Orinoco.

"I found that the temperature grew warmer to such a degree that when we reached the island of Trinidad, the air was pleasant and the land and trees very green and as beautiful as in April in the orchards of Valencia... The Holy Scripture says that Our Lord created Paradise on Earth, that he planted the tree of life from which a source flowed, branching out in four major rivers: the Ganges in India, the Tigris and Euphrates, which separate mountains, form Mesopotamia and flow into Persia, and the Nile, which begins in Ethiopia and flows into the sea at Alexandria... Scholars agree that Paradise on Earth lies in the east. I have already described my feelings about this hemisphere and its form, and I believe that if I were to sail below the equinoctial line toward the highest point, I would find milder temperatures and other differences between the stars

Right:
Brazil. The power and breadth of South America's Orinoco, Amazon, De la Plata, and Parana rivers so impressed Europeans that they were depicted as caricatures on maps of the New World.

Background image:
A Tupinamba family from Brazil. The artist engraved two curiosity objects for Europeans visiting Brazil: a hammock and a pineapple. The friendly air of this couple contrasts with Zacharias Wagner's horrible depictions. Engraving from the *Histoire d'un voyage fait en la terre du Brésil* by Jean de Léry, 1578.

and in the waters. I do not believe that the extreme tip of the height is navigable, nor that water is found there, nor that it is accessible. I am convinced that Paradise on Earth is located here, and no one has access to it without divine intervention…I do not conceive that Paradise on Earth is shaped like a steep mountain, as passages describing it attest, but instead that it lies on top of the summit, at the point I mentioned, the narrow section of the pear, which one gradually ascends by a slope from far away. I believe that no one can reach the top of the summit, as I said, and that this water can come from there, although it is far away, and that the water will flow from where I have just come where it forms a lake. These are the major signs of Paradise on Earth… The extremely mild temperatures lend support to this." Judging his speed to be great as he headed north, he added a few days later: "And this adds to the knowledge that one ascends from there going south, while going north as I was, one descends."

Columbus's letter to the Catholic kings about the third voyage introduced a new and disturbing element into the adventure taking place within territory that was incomparable to what was currently known. The Bible (Genesis II: 8-14) gives strange geographical information about the four great rivers in the world, yet Christians had never been bothered by the inconsistencies. The Near East was undoubtedly far enough away overseas to obfuscate this anomaly. Once rooted, the legend maintaining that it was the torrid heat of the tropical sun that produced gold also contributed in fueling excitement over the marvels of the tropics. Legends such as these were an integral part of the explorers' world, just as Ptolemy's geographical theories, legendary beasts, and Marco Polo's unconfirmed hypotheses were.

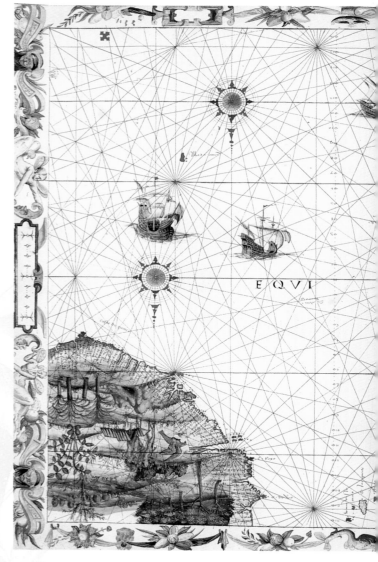

AMERICA

If Grenada had not fallen in 1492, thus spearheading the historical voyage to the west, or if the admiral had perished in the storm on his return voyage,

Portugal inevitably would have discovered America. Two years after Columbus's exploration of the mouth of the Orinoco River and his theories of the proximity of Paradise on Earth, the fleet of Pedro Alvares Cabral, who embarked to establish the Indian empire via the route opened by Vasco da Gama, rebounded off what was Brazil. Following the great *volte* of the South Atlantic, the fleet sailed across the Atlantic with the northeastern trade winds, then caught the westerly winds, which carried it toward the Cape of Good

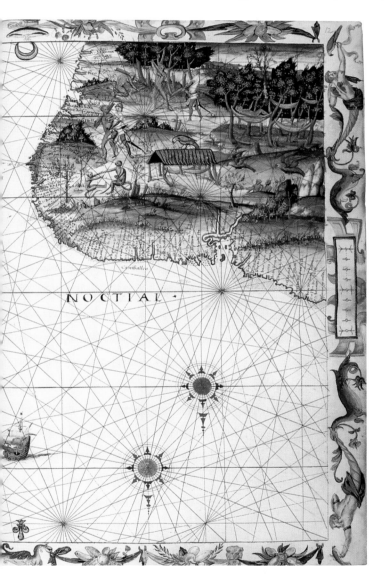

Hope by crossing the Atlantic a second time, this time from west to east. "The following Wednesday morning [April 22, 1500], we encountered birds that we called bone-breaking petrels, and that day at the hour of vespers, we sighted land: first a very high rounded hill south of which were other lower mountains, then a plain covered with vast forests; and the commander named this great hill Mount Pascal, and the land was named True Cross."

The report sent to King Dom Manuel by Pêro Vaz de Caminha, a writer who accompanied Pedro Alvares Cabral, *capitào-mor,* commander in chief of the Indies fleet of 1500, also underscored the strategic interest of the land discovered along the path of the *volte* to the Indies.

This stopover perhaps had already been secretly discovered, although this has never been proven. Whatever the case, the negotiation of clauses of the Treaty of Tordesillas, which divided the world in 1494 between Spain and Portugal, situated Brazil in the Lusitanian half when it was officially discovered, whereas the rest of the two Americas were located in the Spanish hemisphere. As a result of this fifteenth-century treaty, Portuguese is spoken in Brazil and Spanish in Latin America.

"And this land is so pleasant that if we wish to seek to profit from it virtually anything can be cultivated, as water is quite abundant. But the best place to put our energies, in my opinion, is to give salvation to the people. This should be the first seed that Your Highness must sow. And even if all that is possible here is to see it as a stopover for the crossing to Calicut, that will suffice." These brief

Left:
Amerigo Vespucci. Painting
by Antonio Giovanni
Varese, sixteenth century.
Palazzo Farnese, Caprarola.

Bottom left:
Brazilian woman.
Illustration from Zacharias
Wagner's travel log,
circa 1634.

Right:
Brazilian man.
Illustration from Zacharias
Wagner's travel log,
circa 1634.

passages reflect the methodical, gradual nature of the Portuguese undertaking, in sharp contrast to the chaos, clatter, and disorder of Spanish initiatives, which relied largely on improvisation (although they were to become more orderly before long). In 1503, the Casa de Contratación de Indias was created, the Indian Business House, inspired by Portugal's Casa da India.

Cardinal Pierre d'Ailly's *Imago Mundi,* from which the following page is excerpted, was one of Columbus's favorite books. According to the theories of the time, the land which he had discovered access to, North America, was very close to Asia, and was depicted as such on maps until the middle of the sixteenth century. On the other hand, a longstanding belief held that a fourth continent should exist to "counterbalance" Asia, just as Africa did with Europe in the southern hemisphere. This idea was well accepted by discoverers during the great era of exploration. South America was believed to be this new continent.

The most famous of all discoverers was an astonishing character and the subject of great controversy for centuries. Amerigo Vespucci was a Florentine merchant and agent of the Medici family who made four trips to the Americas sailing under the Spanish and then the Portuguese flag. He encountered the leading navigators. Without himself having taking any initiatives, he was named the first Pilot Major by the Casa de Contratación of Seville to oversee the updating of the *Padrón real,* the secret map of the Spanish explorers, and to train pilots. A merchant by profession and navigator by choice, he wrote two letters in the form of travel reports. One was to Lorenzo de' Medici, the other to Pier Soderini, who held what today

In the east, the dwellings of men
stretch far into the distance,
for according to cosmographers,
more than one-half of the Earth's
sphere lies between the western
extremity and that of the Indies.
This is why Pliny maintains that the
Indies form the third part of the
inhabited Earth; and its eastern side,
according to some authors,
approaches ever so slightly the
African extremity. But there is more:
the fourth part of the Earth, and
even the half that lies opposite this
half, must be considered inhabitable
according to the principles of
natural science, just as ours is, and
is not covered with water as is
commonly believed.

Cardinal Pierre d'Ailly, *Imago Mundi*, 1410.

would be considered the mayoralty of Florence. In sum, there were a handful of pages in all. Printing had only recently been developed, and the new art needed new texts, and those by Amerigo Vespucci could draw many readers, who were still less than demanding at the time, given that the author described newly discovered lands. Vespucci was the first narrator of the history of sea exploration to be widely promoted, and for this reason—no other—the author of a humble thirty-two-pages (he had no link in pursuing the discovery) mistakenly gave his name to America.

The first letter set the process in motion. Describing his voyage along South America seeking a passage to the Moluccas (which Magellan would discover twenty years later), Amerigo Vespucci maintained that the land "could be called the New World, for none of his predecessors knew anything about the territories which we see, nor about what the lands contained… I found south of the equator a continent where many valleys are inhabited with many more men and beasts than our Europe is." This was accurate, yet Vespucci had participated only in reconnoitering previously discovered lands, leading people to believe that he was an explorer. His ambiguous writings bolstered his self-inflated importance.

Translated into Latin from the Italian, *Mondus Novus* was the attention-grabbing title of the first of an impressive series of fourteen editions in Latin and a variety of other languages. A general opus on discovery and exploration in Vicenza was published in 1507. This book compiled all existing texts on travel. In addition to the log books by Columbus and Vasco da Gama's travelogue, there were pages from Vespucci's second letter. The elements were grouped together under a Latin title meaning "New World and lands recently discovered by

Left:
Portrait of Amerigo Vespucci. Anonymous, undated.

Bottom left:
Copy of the mappa mundi *Orbis typus universalis juxta hydrographorum traditionem.* This map by Laurentius Frisius (1522) reproduces the original mappa mundi, designed by Martin Waldseemüller and printed at Saint-Dié in 1507. It is complementary to Ptolemy's *Geography.* The name America appeared for the first time on this mappa mundi, as well as on the large planisphere *Universalis Cosmographiae* which Waldseemüller printed the same year.

Right:
Page from the *Imago Mundi* belonging to Columbus. There are some 2,565 footnotes and sidenotes inscribed in the margins of Columbus's reference works. There are 475 in this 1483 edition of the 1410 *Imago Mundi* written by Cardinal Pierre d'Ailly (1350-1420). It is from the eighth chapter, *The Quantity of Inhabitable Land.* Columbus notes in the margins his own theories that often contradict those of leading scholars.

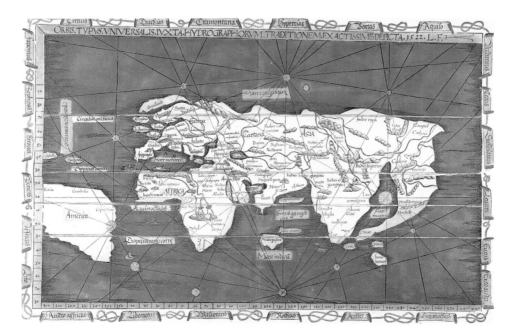

ꝗ durat unus dies in uno loco per unū mēsem Jn alio per duos Jn alio
per tres vel plꝰ ꞇ ꝓporcionaliter est lōgior illa nox hyemis. Sexta ē
ꝗ illi qui habitarēt recte sub polo haberēt per mediū ām Solē sup orizō
tem ꞇ ōtinuū diē ꞇ per aliud dimidiū cōtinuam nocte Et ita si uocemus
diē totū tēpus quo Sol ē super orizonte nō haberēt toto āno nisi unum
diem ꞇ nocte. Et sicut dictū est de ista medietate terre que ē versꝰ poluꝝ
articū siℓr itelligendū est de alia medietate vsus ātarticū ꞇ habitatori
bus eiꝰ Et hec ōnia sine alia ꝓbatione exēplariter patēt i spa materiali.

De quantitate terre habitabilis   Capitulū octauū

AD inuestigandū quātitatem habitationis terre itelligendū est ꝗ ha
bitatio dupliciter ōsiderat. Vno mō respectu celi.s. ꝗntū propter
Solē pōt habitari ꞇ ꝗtum nō. ꞇ de hoc superiꝰ generaliter ē satis dictū
Alio mō ōsideratꞅ respectu aque.s. ꝗtum aꝗ ipediat. ꞇ de hoc nūc ē cōside
randuꝝ. De quo varie sunt opiniones sapientū. Nā Ptholomeꝰ libro de
dispōne spere. vult ꝗ fere sexta pars terre ē habitabilis propter aquā. ꞇ
totū residuū ē coopertū aꝗ. Et ita i Algamesti libro .ii. ponit ꝗ habita
tio nota nō ē nisi in quarta terre.s. in qua habitamꝰ Cuiꝰ lōgitudo ē ab
oriēte i occidēs. ꞇ ē medietas eꝗnoxialis Et eiꝰ latitudo ē ab equinoxiali
i polū. ꞇ est ꝗrta coluri. Sꝫ Aristotiles in fine libri celi ꞇ mūdi. vult ꝗ
plꝰ habitetꞅ ꝗ quarta. Et Auerroys hoc cōfirmat Et dicit Aristotiles ꝗ
mare paruū est iter finē Hyspanie a pte occidētis/ ꞇ iter principiū Jndie
a parte orientis. Et nō loquitꞅ de Hyspania citeriori/ ꝗ nūc hyspania cō
muniter nominatur. sed de Hyspania vlteriori que nūc Africa dicitur.
de qua certi auctores loquuntur. vt Plinius Orosius ꞇ Ysidorus. Jn
super Seneca libro quinto naturalium dicit ꝗ mare est nauigabile i pau
cis diebus si ventus sit conueniens. Et Plinius docet in naturalibus li
bro secūdo. ꝗ nauigatum est a sinu Arabico vsꝗ ad gades Herculis nō
multum magno tempore. vnde ex hiis ꞇ multis aliis rationibꝰ de quibus
magis tangam cum loquar de Oceano cōcludunt aliqui apparēter ꝗ ma
re non ē tātuꝝ ꝗ possit coopertire tres quartas terre. Accedit ad hoc auc
toritas Esore libro suo quarto. dicentis ꝗ sex partes terre sunt habita
te ꞇ septima est cooperta aquis. cuius libri auctoritatez sancti habuerūt
in reuerētia. ꞇ veritates sacras per eum confirmarunt. Et ideo videtꞅ ꝗ
licet habitatio nota Ptholomeo et eius sequacibus sit coartata ifra ꝗr
tam vnam plus tamen est habitabile. Et Aristotiles circa hoc plus potu
it nosse auxilio Alexandri. Et Seneca auxilio Neronis. qui ad inuestigā
dum dubia huius mundi fuerunt solliciti. Sicut de Alexandro testātur
Plinius libro octauo. et etiam Solinus. Et de Nerone narrat Seneca
libro de naturalibꝰ. Vn illis magis videtꞅ credendū ꝗ Ptholomeo vℓ eti
am ꝗ Albategni ꝗ adhuc minꝰ pōit ē habitabile. videℓz solū duodecimā
ptem. sꝫ deficit in ꝓbatiōe sicut posset ostēdi/ sed breuitatis causa transeo

S. augustinus de ciuitate dei

Alberico [sic] Vespucci of Florence." Thus the unwarranted promotion of a slim work of sixteen pages, of which only a few descriptive pages about the mores and customs of the Indians bore any interest. "And if I wished to recount what I saw along this coast and what we passed by, still as many pages would not be enough." This taciturn author went on to explain: "These people inhabiting these lands, I encountered and observed so many of their customs and ways of life that I am not concerned with recounting them, because Your Magnificence will know that in each of my voyages I noted the most curious of things and I reduced it all into one volume as geography and I entitled it: *The Four Days.*" The promised work never saw the day.

Martin Waldseemüller, one of a group of humanists known as the Gymnasium Vosagense in Saint-Dié, prepared with his colleagues a new edition of Ptolemy's *Geography,* which incorporated the latest Iberian discoveries in Africa and the western Atlantic. Waldseemüller was working on a contemporary world map, based on the Greek geography of Ptolemy, and he had read of Vespucci's travels and knew that the New World was indeed two continents. In honor of Vespucci's discovery of the new fourth portion of the world, Waldseemüller printed a wood block map with the name "America" spread across the southern continent of the New World in 1507. Within a few years, Waldseemüller changed his mind about the name for the New World but it was too late. The name America had stuck. The power of the printed word was too powerful to retract.

FRANCESCA

Spain established its New World empire with the conquest of Mexico in 1519 and Peru in 1532, which allowed the mining of argentiferous lead in Peru, Mexico, and Bolivia, and gold in Columbia and Costa Rica from the mid-sixteenth century on. Thus began the adventure of the gold fleets, Spanish galleons, and the world of corsairs, pirates, and buccaneers. Beginning in the late fifteenth century, European maritime expeditions explored the coasts of America, north of New Spain. After the expeditions of John and Sebastian Cabot (John was from Genoa, and Sebastian was born in Venice), who were in the service of Henry VII of England, Gaspar Corte Real and his brother Miguel of Portugal disappeared during the exploration of the area surrounding

Labrador, looking for the existence of a passage to India via the American northwest.

The first explorer sailing to America in the service of France was of Italian origin. Giovanni da Verrazano came from a family of Florentine traders which had settled in Lyon. He set sail from Dieppe aboard the *Dauphine* to look for a passage to India. In spring of 1524, he explored the American coast from what is currently North Carolina to Maine, claiming the land for Francis I. He proposed naming the area Francesca. Despite his adamant demand for a share in the "Testament d'Adam" dividing the world between Spain and Portugal, the French king had too much to do in Italy to challenge Spain's claims to the New World. Francesca remained a mere proposal, appearing on a few dozen maps and mappae mundi until the mid-sixteenth century.

Giovanni da Verrazano sent the report on the *Dauphine's* voyage to Francis I upon his arrival in Dieppe in 1524. In mid-April, he came upon a huge estuary, "a highly pleasant place, dominated by two small hills between which a broad river flowed all the way to the sea. The mouth was deep, we determined the tide to be eight feet, and all cargo ships could ply the waters. After mooring near the coast in a sheltered area, we hesitated to venture farther without first sending out reconnaissance missions. Sailing the launch upriver, we entered a land that we found densely inhabited. The people (as those whom we had met), dressed in brightly colored bird feathers, greeted us gaily, shouting in admiration and indicating the safest place for pulling ashore. We ascended the river as far as a half-league inland, where we saw an extremely beautiful lake approximately three leagues in circumference. Some thirty little boats were sailing to and fro over the entire lake, carrying an infinite number of people heading from shore to shore to see us. Suddenly, as is common in sailing, a gust of wind blew in from

the sea, and we were forced to return on board, leaving this land with a great deal of regret, given the convenience and contemplation it offered us, and having estimated that it was rich in precious resources, with the hills being a source of minerals. We named it *Angoulême,* after the name of the county which you received for a lesser fortune."

The discovery of the site was long attributed to Henry Hudson, who came upon it and explored it in 1609 for the Dutch Trading Company; the river discovered by Verazzano was named after Hudson. The Dutch relied upon these indications in setting

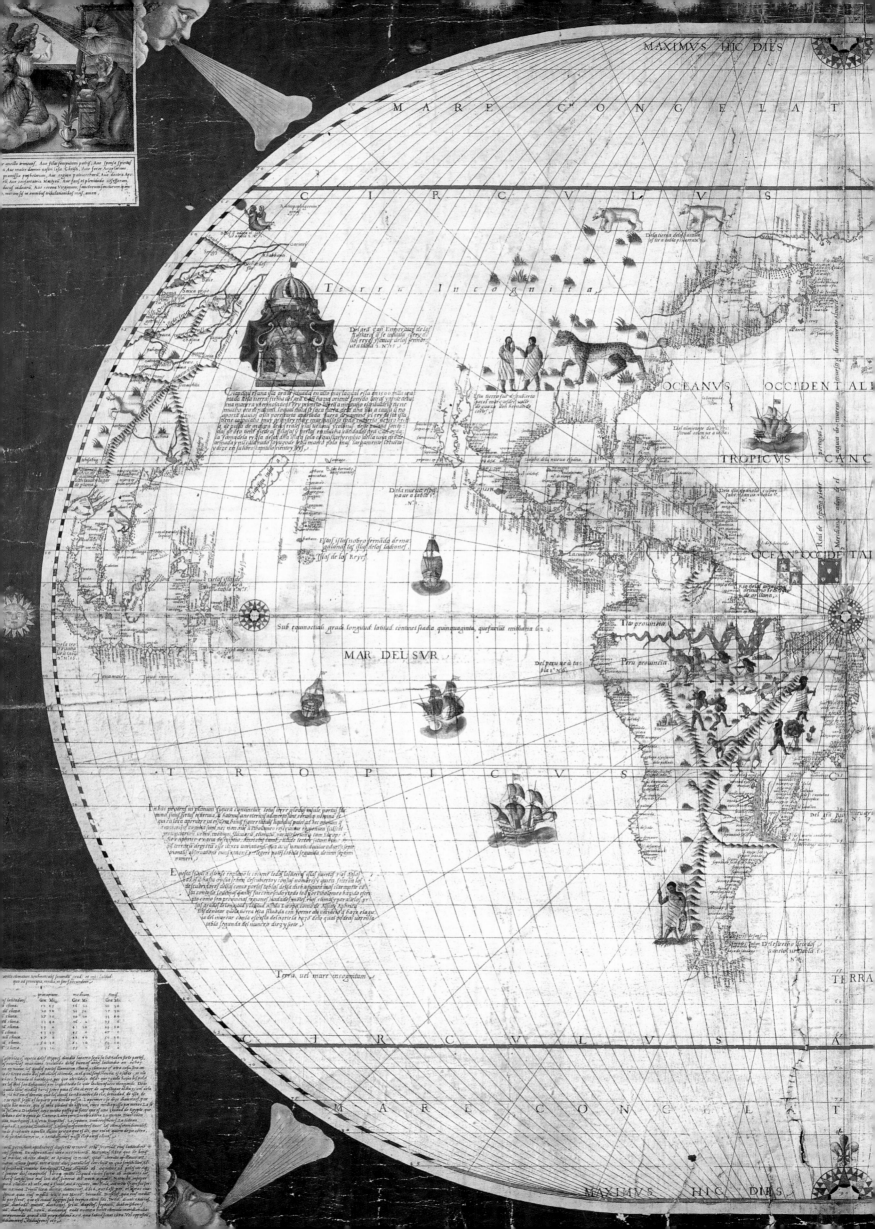

Left:
Spain's western part of
Sebastian Cabot's 1544
planisphere, engraved in
1559 by Clement Adams.

Right:
Natives from the Maragnon
River. Six Indian chiefs
were brought back from
Maranhào (Brazil) by
Daniel de La Ravardière
and François de Razilly to
be presented to Louis XIII.
Their arrival generated
a great deal of enthusiasm.
Illustration from
Géographie du Monde by
Artus Fonnant, 1633.
Taken from an engraving
by Pierre Firens (1613)
from a drawing by Joachim
Dubiert, entitled *Natives
Brought to France to be
Instructed in the Catholic
Faith.*

up the colony of Nieuw Nederlandt on Nut Island (Governors Island) in 1624
and purchasing Manhattan two years later, founding Nieuw Amsterdam. New
Angoulême is now named New York.

The *Dauphine* continued its exploration. "Having hoisted up the anchor, we
headed east, following the direction of the coast. We sailed along without losing
sight of it for a moment, for eighty leagues. We discovered an island that was
rectangular in shape, some ten leagues off the continent, its width comparable to
that of Rhodes, covered with hills and trees and greatly populated." Francesca
was soon covered in Anglo-Saxon toponyms. Verazzano named part of the
eastern coast Arcadia. Although the area was far, far away from the pastoral
region of Ancient Greece, Verazzano was smitten by "the beauty of its trees."
Perhaps Rhode Island is the island that so resembles Rhodes, which he had
dedicated to Louise, the mother of the king of France.

Preceding double page:
*Which tells of the arrival
of a French boat, which
bought Brazilwood and
cotton from the natives
and on which I would have
willingly boarded had
God so permitted.* This is
another episode from
Hans Staden's ill-fated
adventure. Hand-colored
engraving by Théodore de
Bry, from a wood engraving
and story by Hans Staden.
Grands Voyages, 1592.

Left:
*Africa and America Helping
Europe.* William Blake
(1757-1827) made this
print of the three Graces.
It is rather cynical,
considering that Europe
at the time was in the
midst of protests against
the African slave trade,
a direct consequence of
the agricultural exploitation
of the Americas.

Right:
Inhabitant of the *Terra
Australis Incognita* (or
Unidentified Southern
Land). This was still
a legendary land mass,
which explorers had not
yet linked to the scraps
of information about the
continent that would
be named Australia,
discovered by the Dutch.
Géographie du Monde,
by Artus Fonnant, 1633.

Once the initial enthusiasm of Columbus's discovery was over, the colonization of what would become America became problematic; indeed, Columbus was cursed for many long years by the *conquistadores.* Their situation was as perilous as those of the sailors aboard ships heading for India. A few centuries later, the voyagers who traveled to the Antarctic in search of the legendary *Terra Australis Incognita* experienced the same hell. Given the social and economic context of Europe through the nineteenth century, the feverish desire for a better future, easy wealth, and indescribable happiness somewhere in an exotic paradise offered an enduring dream to counter the miserable existence of everyday life. This myth was powerful enough to maintain the momentum of the discovery voyages and the exploration of the Indies—despite the hardship of the infernal torments encountered on difficult routes that sometimes led nowhere, or even to destinies worse than the ones left behind.

Christopher Columbus had no idea of the importance of his discovery, and he devoted his life to achieving some degree of prestige. In comparison with the immense revenues pouring into the Portuguese coffers from the East Indies, his discovery—the West Indies—cut a poor figure: the lands were costly, complicated, and tumultuous. Columbus appears to have been a somewhat annoying character, with swaggering ways, insufficient navigational skills, inept administration of the empire he had discovered, and excessive attention to his name—which has become a symbol for the discovery of the United States of America itself, although he never set foot there. In the end, however, he was the one man who, alone against everyone, stood up to the scientists on the Spanish commission. His shrewd intelligence of philosophy and the dogma of his time, his enterprising spirit, his courage, and perhaps his naiveté propelled him far beyond the other discoverers. It was of little importance that he was wrong about almost everything: Columbus was the only discoverer in history to have supported, defended, and pursued his own theory to its logical outcome, against all odds. He did not discover the Indies, but he did something even better: he found the legendary El Dorado, although no one would know this until some twenty years after he died—not exactly in disgrace, but certainly forgotten.

Sometimes, ships returning from the Indies received a poignant, silent welcome. The crews aboard the ships captained by the brothers Jean and Raoul Parmentier of Dieppe were an example; a handful of survivors returned from Sumatra as if from hell, humiliated, miserable, and battered to the depths of their souls.

As opposed to America, a continent that appeared unexpectedly out of nowhere, the myth of the *Terra Australis Incognita* persisted, despite evidence refuting its existence. Armchair geographers affirmed that it had to be inhabitable and fertile, contradicting the opinion offered by sailors, who viewed it, at best, as a few desolate, rocky patches of land with an unbearable climate. Kerguelen had allowed himself to be duped by the philosophical vision of a prosperous colony beyond the Roaring Forties. He paid a heavy price for his convictions; when the subpolar climate refused to comply with the dreams of powerful theoreticians, Kerguelen was punished and spent several years in prison. Dozens of scientists and sailors on the exploratory trips during the Age of Enlightenment lost their lives due to misunderstandings and incomprehension between cultures that were fundamentally opposed. Their leaders knew by experience what to expect from men, and their experience at sea often turned them bitter in the face of the pontifical speeches of the humanists back home.

The discoverers, in the larger sense of the term—whom the Portuguese named *descobrimento*, which means more than *descoberta* by including the cultural significance of the act of discovering—all faced a brutal contrast between the theories of science, politics, fortune, and philosophy and the harsh reality in remote worlds. They were special envoys from the West to the new worlds, with the unprecedented privilege of traveling around the Earth. Hence, they suffered all the errors in judgement in European knowledge, while taking responsibility for all the setbacks.

CASTAWAYS OF THE NEW WORLD

The town of Isabela, the first in the New World, was founded in the spring of 1494 by Christopher Columbus on a coastal plain of Hispaniola (Haiti-Dominican Republic), a site that pleased him for its setting and its strategic possibilities. This location turned out to a bad choice, however, as it was unhealthy. Ironically, in the mid-eighteenth century, the Portuguese were forced to abandon their Indian capital for the same reasons, after a new and particularly virulent epidemic struck the inhabitants. They retreated to the coast at Panaji, where the air was cleaner.

Las Casas described the situation in Isabela: "The men suddenly started to fall ill and, due to the lack of care we were able to provide, many of them died. So many, in fact, that there was barely a single man among the hidalgos and the indigenous people, however strong, who was not struck by these terrible fevers. The work was almost the same for everyone, as can be imagined by anyone who knows what it means to populate a new land, especially in these regions. It was more laborious than in any other time or any other place. Added to their pain was

F. Maii.

9.

 BSERVATIS multis ejus regionis fluminibus, tandem itum est in eam sententiam, potius ad flumen Maii deligendas esse sedes, quàm ad aliud ullum flumen: quia jam animadverterant illud præ reliquis milio & farina abundare, præter aurum & argentum quod istic in prima navigatione repertum est: cursum igitur ad id flumen direxerunt, in quo cùm navigassent ad locum quendam monti vicinum, commodior æstimatus est ille locus ad arcem condendam, quam ullus alius hactenus ab ipsis conspectus. Postridie summo diluculo, fusis ad Deum precibus, & actis gratijs de felici in eam provinciam adventu, omnes alacres sunt redditi: deinde plana area in triquetram formam dimensa, singuli manum operi admovere cœperunt; alij terram evertendo, alij fasces ex virgultis cæsis componendo, alij vallum conficiendo: nemo enim adfuit qui palam, serram, securim, aliudve instrumentum non haberet, cùm ad arbores cædendas, tum ad arcem instruendam, eaque diligentia adhibita est, ut brevi opus procederet.

the great despair and sadness at being so far away from their countries and especially without any hopes of remedying this situation. They were also frustrated in their desire to find gold and other treasures, which had motivated their decision to come to these lands. The admiral fell ill like the others, as he had been performing his incomparable work at sea by depriving himself of sleep, as is often required by this art that he practices. And the admiral also carried the responsibility for the pilots who usually navigated in lands they had traveled many times before, for the simple reason that in this new and unprecedented era, he was the only one who knew the route. As a result, the well-being of the entire fleet rested on his shoulders. In addition to the work that was greater for him than for anyone else, everyone expected him to explain how to finish any project that had been started."

Nevertheless, Isabela rose from the ground, with houses and a church, in which thirteen priests celebrated the first high mass on Epiphany. On January 30, 1494, a message from the admiral to the Catholic sovereigns, given to Antonio de Torres, captain of the Marie-Galante (who had been appointed alcade, or mayor, or Isabela) listed their most urgent requirements. "With the small number of healthy men who remain, we work every day to enclose the town for defense and to place provisions in a safe place. All this should take a few days, as we are only building a dry-stone enclosure… You shall tell Their Highnesses, as has already been said, that the causes of such a widespread illness are due to a change in water and air, as we see that it is gradually spreading to all of us, but that few are in real danger.

Consequently, maintaining the health of these people depends, after God, on providing them with the food that they are accustomed to eating in Spain, because Their Highnesses can get nothing of the men who are here or those who are to come if they are not in good health. These provisions should continue until we have obtained the produce from all we have seeded and planted, by which I mean wheat, barley and vines—which we did not tend well this year because we were not able to settle in earlier; as soon as we did, the few laborers we had fell ill.

And even had they remained healthy, they would not have been able to do very much as there were so few animals, and these were so thin and exhausted. Despite this, however, we did sow some seeds, more to test the earth, which seems to be wonderful, that in expectation of any solution to our needs... You will say that a large share of the wine that the fleet carried on this voyage was spilled, and most men say that this was the fault of the poor workmanship by the coopers from Seville—yet it is wine that we miss more than anything else now, and we would like to have more. Although we have hardtack and wheat for some time, it is nevertheless necessary to send a reasonable quantity to us, as the route is long and we can not receive supplies every day. The same is true for meat, by which I mean lard and other cured meats, which must be better than the supplies we brought with us on this trip. We also need live sheep—preferable male and female lambs—several small calves and a few small heifers sent to us whenever any ship comes our way; in addition, jackasses and jennies, and mares to reproduce and work in the fields, as there are no animals here that can serve and help man."

The feverish gentlemen, whose sweat- and rain-soaked clothes did little to hide their emaciated bodies, discovered the hard labor of a farming colonist in a country where nothing yet existed. This existence was quite different from the promised gold deposits, which were supposed to be so abundant that they were to have gathered this precious ore by the handful. It was extremely expensive to maintain a colony here. Even though their normal lives in Spain were austere, these colonists were less to living in discomfort and want than were sailors. Columbus's plea for help listed their requirements like a litany. "To encourage our people here, we must do everything possible so that [the two caravels] return sometime in the month of May, so that before summer begins, our people see that their provisions have been replenished; and especially that the sick people receive the goods we lack, particularly raisons, sugar, almonds, honey and rice, which should have been sent in large quantities, and wine—of which we received very little. This small amount has been consumed, as has most of the medicine brought from there, due to the large number of ill people."

He followed this list with a series of recommendations suggesting that pensions be paid to a few particularly deserving people, and that the balance of payment be distributed to those who had come to Hispaniola assured of instant wealth only to find themselves in poverty. "More than two hundred people came here without any

payment, including those who are of great service; we put them forward as examples to others to whom we ask as much... Their Highnesses must let us know if these two hundred people who arrived without payment will receive money as have the others, provided they work well. They are indeed useful in this early period, as I have already said."

In addition to the usual provisions and medicine, he also urgently requested shoes and leather for shirts, doublets, fabrics, clothes, breeches and cloth, two hundred breastplates, one hundred blunderbusses, one hundred crossbows and a large amount of munitions, fifty casks of molasses from Madeira, ten crates of sugar, as well as gold-panners and miners from Almaden, beasts of burden, and farming implements.

In the enthusiasm of Columbus's first return journey, everyone had forgotten that the goal was to construct a forward base from scratch, a project similar to the construction of the orbiting space station in our own time. Hispaniola would turn out to be an investment that provided unprecedented profits, but for the time being, the expenses it incurred came at a bad moment. Columbus had neglected to describe in his project the sweat and tears leading to the road of wealth and to the glory of God and Spain. Starting in 1497, there were no longer enough volunteers. Instead, convicts who opted to travel to Hispaniola had their sentences commuted.

THEY THEN BEGAN TO HATE ME

Columbus offered a simple suggestion to pay for the colony's upkeep and development and to make profitable an undertaking which, lacking valuable natural resources, was bringing nothing to the treasury. "You shall tell Their Highnesses that, for the good of the souls of the aforesaid cannibals, and even for the inhabitants here, it came to us that later we will send them something better, which would serve Their Highnesses: ... The convoy ships could be paid in cannibal slaves; they are ferocious people but vigorous and strongly built, and very intelligent. Removed from their inhumane conditions, they would, believe us, be the best of slaves and would lose their bad habits as soon as they had left their land. We could capture many of them with these store ships that we are thinking of

Native Caribbeans. The author was promoting his version of the "noble savages," who were warriors, but civilized. Illustration from the *Géographie du Monde* by Artus Fonnant, 1633.

Right:
On the military discipline of Outina's warriors. The scene details the practices of war among the Florida natives. It offers a sharp contrast with the vision on the preceding page, opposing the actual experiences of travelers with armchair philosophy. Hand-colored engraving by Théodore de Bry, from Jacques Lemoyne de Morgues. Ribault and Laudonnière's voyage to Florida (1562-1565). *Grands Voyages,* 1591.

REGE Saturioua ad bellum proficiscente, ejus milites nullum ordinem servant, sed sparsi hinc inde discurrunt alij alios sequentes. Contra ejus hostis Holata Outina, cujus jam memini, quod multorum Regum Regem significat, longè eò potentior subditorum nume- ro & divitijs, progreditur servatis ordinibus veluti instructa acie, solus in medio agmine consistens, rubro colare pictus: agminis alæ sive cornua ex adolescentibus constant, quorum maximè agiles, rubro etiam colore picti cursorum & exploratorum munere funguntur, ad hostium copias explorandas: nam horum vestigia perinde naribus percipiunt, atque canis feræ alicujus, & cognitis hostium vestigijs statim ad exercitum significatum recurrunt. Porro ut tubis & tympanis nostri homines in exercitu utuntur ad significandum quid facto opus sit: sic apud eos præcones sunt, qui certis clamoribus indicant quan- do subsistendum aut progrediendum, hosti obviam eundum, aut aliquod militare munus obeundum. Post Solis occasum subsistunt, nec unquam pugnare solent. Castra autem ponere volentes per decurias distribuuntur, maximè strenuos ab alijs segregantes: delecto à Rege Castrorum loco in agris vel syluis ad noctem traducen- dam, & illo jam cœnato & solo sedente, castrorum metatores decem strenuiorum decurias in orbem circum Regem collocant: circiter decem inde passus aliæ viginti decuriæ etiam in orbem eos claudunt: viginti verò ab illis passus, aliæ quadraginta decuriæ collocantur, & ita deinceps decuriarum & passuum numerum au- gendo pro exercitus copia & magnitudine.

building here... As for the slaves we ship back, Their Highnesses could, on their arrival, deduct their fees from their sale value."

The Spanish sovereigns responded coolly to this suggestion, although not for moral reasons—as the New World would transform the slave trade into a thriving industry—or for fear of releasing cannibals in Spain. They first wanted to decide if these Indians were slaves or vassals. "The decision on this point has been set aside for the moment pending new proposals from you. Let the admiral write to us with

How gold is found in the rivers flowing down the Apalacty Hills. This gold-panning scene in the Appalachian rivers is a discreet allusion to the great question troubling the explorers in the Americas. The author added, enviously:

suggestions." Las Casas noted that in 1499 he witnessed the queen's wrath when she saw slaves being distributed on the wharves of Cadix to gentlemen returning from the West Indies. She apparently ordered that they be returned immediately to Hispaniola.

In September 1494, when Columbus returned to Isabela from his exploratory trip to Cuba, Jamaica and the southerern coast of the Dominican Republic, he discovered a tense situation. His brothers Diego and especially Bartolomeu, appointed *adelantado* or governor, had not been able to control the colony, even with the use of force. The relationship between the Spanish, obsessed with gold and

"The Spanish have managed to capture for themselves the wealth from these places." Hand-colored engraving by Théodore de Bry, from Jacques Lemoyne de Morgues. Ribault and Laudonnière's voyage to Florida (1562-1565). *Grands Voyages,* 1591.

Trophies and ritual ceremonies celebrating the defeat of the enemy. Hand-colored engraving by Théodore de Bry, from Jacques Lemoyne de Morgues. Ribault and Laudonnière's voyage to Florida (1562-1565). Grands Voyages, 1591.

women, and the Arawaks had become explosive. An escalation of brutalities, insults, forced labor, deportation, slavery, murder, executions, massacres, skirmishes, and pitched battles was the inexorable sequence of events in the New World. The gold tribute imposed by the admiral on the Indians had completely destabilized their economy. The little gold they owned had been obtained using simple gathering techniques, essentially the same way they obtained mother-of-pearl and parrot feathers. Once their initial stock was depleted, the tribute forced

them to become gold-diggers and to abandon their fields. Two-thirds of the Indian population died in two years. The process of "the destruction of the Indies," as denounced by Las Casas, was underway. Enthusiasm had dropped in Spain as well, and the Catholic monarchs started to entertain serious doubts about the future of their colony. When Juan Aguado disembarked at Isabela with a mission to inquire about Hispaniola, Columbus understood that he needed to return urgently to Spain to defend his work and his convictions. He arrived at Cadix in June of 1496. The admiral managed to correct the deplorable view of the West Indies project, although he faced indifference from the court, preoccupied by the dynastic

Your Exalted Highnesses, when I came here,
I brought many men to conquer these lands,
men who were looking for jobs and who told me
that they would work very hard. But this
was not the case; quite the contrary. They came
merely because they were convinced that they
could pick up gold by the shovelful, and that
spices were lying about in piles along the entire
stretch of the riverbank, and that all they
had to do was load it onto the ships; their
cupidity so blinded them that they no longer
even considered that the gold, if there was any,
would be in mines, like other metals, and that
this gold had to be found and extracted, and that
the spices had to be collected and treated. I had
told them this in Seville, as many of them
approached me, and I was aware of their
thoughts; I tried to explain to them the suffering
of those who leave to populate new, remote
lands. To this, they all replied that they were
coming for this very reason and to find fame.
But because they did not really believe it,
as I have already said, when they arrived and
saw that I had been telling the truth, and that
that their greed would not be satisfied, they
wanted to return immediately, without
understanding the hardships of conquering a
country. And because I would not accede to their
demands, they then began to hate me.

Christopher Colombus, "Letter to the Catholic Kings,"
May 1499.

strategies of forging an alliance with the Netherlands and war over the control of Italian territories.

He left on his third voyage in 1498, reassured that Isabella of Castile's friendship would ensure further prestige and higher offices. Yet once he discovered the mouth of the Orinoco River, the admiral's privileges were in fact circumvented, as a different expedition was ordered to explore this region. When Columbus reached Hispaniola, the island was in the midst of an open rebellion, triggered by the premature announcement of his disgrace. Francisco Roldán, the *alcade* (mayor) and the admiral's trusted right-hand man, was leading a band of mutineers. They were pacified, although only temporarily, by a distribution of land.

Deeply wounded, Columbus expressed his bitterness to the Catholic sovereigns during his third trip to the Americas, and decided to go on the offensive to defend himself and his work, which was in serious jeopardy. Perhaps he was also seeking a way to justify to himself the trivial nature of his extravagant promises, to convince himself of the legitimacy of the foolhardy promises that had opened a Pandora's box, from which so many calamities were now escaping.

THE STORM

Commander Francisco de Bobadilla landed on August 23, 1500 at the port of Santo Domingo and immediately took over the situation in the name of the crown. This bombshell rocked the settlement of Hispaniola and stunned its founder. The disgrace was total and overwhelming.

"The second day after he arrived, he proclaimed himself governor, created magistrates, proceeded with executions, and pronounced the end of the gold tax and tithes, and generally, on everything for a period of twenty years, which is, as I said, the age of a man. He announced that he had arrived to pay everyone, even those who had not entirely fulfilled their service and that, as far as I was concerned, he was ordered to send me back in chains as well as my brothers—which he did—and that never again would I return there, nor any member of my family. And he said a thousand dishonest and discourteous things about me. All this happened the day after he arrived, as I said, and when I was far away, without any knowledge of him or of his arrival. He had a large number of blank documents signed by Their Highnesses; these were filled out and sent to the *alcade* as well as to others in his entourage, granting them favors and offices. And he never sent either a letter or messenger to me, nor to this day has given me anything. Let Your Grace imagine what anyone in my position would have thought! To honor and shower favors on he who wants to steal Their Highnesses' domain and who did so much damage and harm; drag through the mud he who protected them from such peril! When I learned this, I thought that this was someone like Hojeda or one of the others. But I controlled myself when I learned from the monks that it was, in fact, Their

Highnesses who had sent him." Columbus wrote this letter to Juana de Torres, nurse to Prince Don Juan, aboard the ship that was bringing him back, in chains, to Spain.

The new governor had pushed things too far, and Columbus did the same, refusing to remove his chains until he had received a royal order to do so—gambling that the scandal would restore his reputation. Called to Grenada, he was treated with honors, but his protector, Queen Isabella, had given up defending her cumbersome admiral. Nicolas de Ovando set sail to take over the position as governor of the islands and the Indies, while Yanez Pinzon and Alonso de Hojeda were named administrators of the mainland of this earthly paradise.

The wheel had turned. Authorized to undertake a fourth voyage in an attempt to straighten out the geography of these complicated Indies, Columbus set sail one last time from Cadix, in 1502. This time, his goal was to find a passage to Calicut (from which Vasco da Gama had just returned) at all costs. The new governor refused to let him make a stop at Santo Domingo. He also ignored the admiral's advice concerning a hurricane—which the Arawaks called a *urucan*—that Columbus said was imminent. In the port, the fleet was getting ready to set sail for Spain with the royal treasure. The violent winds sank some twenty ships. Among the five hundred men who died were the Commander Bobadilla, who had been called back to Spain, and the rebel Francisco Roldán, who was to be judged. Columbus and his captains, familiar with the seas of the Antilles, managed to save their caravels.

On this fourth and last trip Columbus suffered illness, storms, torrential rains, shipwrecks, hostility from Indians, and a mutiny by members of his exhausted crew. He was desperately seeking some evidence of a western passage that would lead to the realm of the Great Khan. As he sailed along Honduras, he thought he was following the coast of China or Cambodia. The disabled expedition

Christopher Columbus's signature at the bottom of a letter dated April 2, 1502, sent to officers in Genoa.
This is another version of the esoteric signature of the "Bearer of Christ," "God chose the admiral, my father, to be a sort of apostle predestined for the great things that he accomplished," his son Ferdinand wrote later.

took shelter in Jamaica. The ailing admiral returned to Sanlúcar on November 7, 1503, after a campaign that had lasted two and a half years.

The following year, he wrote several touching letters to his son from Seville, complaining bitterly that he was no longer receiving the pensions that he had been promised. "It seems to me that we must copy, in good handwriting, the paragraph of the letter Their Highnesses sent to me, in which they said that they would keep all the promises they made to me and would give you possession of everything. Give it to them with another letter, which mentions my illness, and that it is impossible for me to go kiss their royal feet and hands; and how the Indies are being lost and are under fire from a thousand sides; and how I have not received and receive nothing of the annuity they owe me; that no one dares to claim it, and that I am living off loans."

Isabella of Castile, his protector, had just died on November 26, six days earlier. Columbus himself passed away on May 20, 1506 in Valladolid. His remains, placed in the crypt of the charterhouse of La Cuevas near Seville, started a long peregrination in 1536. Transferred to Santo Domingo in 1536, where they remained eighteen years amid total indifference, they were placed with ceremony in the cathedral. When the island became French in 1795, his ashes were sent to Santiago de Cuba. One wonders about the remaining contents of the discoverer's cenotaph, which is now honored in the cathedral of Seville.

THE MYTH OF THE *TERRA AUSTRALIS INCOGNITA*

The *Terra Australis Incognita* was created by Greek geographers who felt they needed to find an equilibrium for the Earth in space, to balance the *oekoumène,* the known and inhabited world, with the *antichtone,* its counterweight in the southern hemisphere. The northwest coast of New Guinea had been identified by the Portuguese in the first few decades of the sixteenth century; it seemed as if this land could belong to the southern continent, which appeared widely on mappi mundi and had acquired a quasi-official status among the great cartographers. It was said to have all the characteristics of a magical site. This hidden continent should have had abundant precious metals, stones, and rare wood, along with strange animals, and kind and gentle people. The Bible accredited this persistent idea. "And King Solomon made a navy of ships in Eziongeber, which is beside Eloth, on the shore of the Red Sea, in the land of Edom. And Hiram sent in the navy his servants, shipmen that had knowledge of the sea, with the servants of Solomon. And they came to Ophir, and fetched from thence gold, four hundred and twenty talents, and brought it to King Solomon." (Book of I Kings 9:26-28)

As the land of Ophir obviously was not in Arabia, nor on the Indian coast, nor even in the spice islands, it had to be located somewhere farther to the south. According to an Incan tradition, an immense country stretched southwest of Peru.

Left:
Map of the Cape of
Good Hope and the *Terra
Australis Incognita.*
*Cosmographie Universelle
selon les navigateurs
tant anciens que modernes*
by Guillaume le Testu,
1556.

Right:
Red parrot and dodo.
This large flightless bird,
native to the Indian
Ocean, was exterminated
in the eighteenth century.
Gouache by William
Hodges, illustrator and
painter aboard Cook's
second voyage, circa 1773.

Following double page:
Plan of the port of
Callao in Peru, sixteenth
century. The gold and
silver ingots from Peru
were loaded at Callao,
Lima's port, and in Arica,
on ships in the Pacific
fleet. They were then
transferred to mule trains
which crossed the
Isthmus of Panama to
Porto Bello, where they
were loaded on the
Fleets of gold.
Anonymous Spanish chart,
late sixteenth century.

Several Spanish expeditions sought the Solomon Islands from Peru, traveling via the multitude of islands and atolls in the immense South Pacific, most often in extremely dangerous conditions, until they discovered the Marquesas Islands and the Santa Cruz Islands. A semblance of a colony survived several hellish months here. The pilot of this last expedition, Pedro Fernandes de Queirós, managed to convince Philip III of Spain that the Santa Cruz, New Guinea, and the Solomon Islands, which remained elusive to the navigator, were situated at the edge of the southern continent.

Queirós was deeply mystical and set sail from Callao in December 1605 to settle a Christian colony on Antarctica. Wandering according to the will of God, the ships landed at Vanuatu in May of 1606. In a delirium of enthusiasm, their leader founded the port of Vera Cruz in the bay of San Felipe y Santiago, where the city of Neuva Jerusalem would be built. The land he had claimed, which reached as far as the South Pole, was named Australia del Espiritu Santo. The colonists abandoned it less than three weeks later, as they were worried about the reaction of the indigenous peoples (indeed, the Melanasians remained cannibals for a long time), and they were made ill by the fish they caught in the lagoon. Today, this is named Espiritu Santo or Santo. It is only the largest of the Vanuatu Islands (formerly New Hebrides). Separated from his leader by the perils of the sea, Luiz Vaez de Torres displayed great courage in his difficult crossing of the strait that now bears his name. He confirmed that New Guinea was an island and, unknowingly, sailed just past the coast of Australia.

Seña de las ormigas al Sur.

Señas delas ormigas al Sueste.

Pto. de Ancon de Rodas

R. de Caraballo.

Sarallon de Da. franCa.

Los Pescadores.

Las Ormigas con la Ya. del Callao estan Sesueste oemorueste a Siette Leguas.

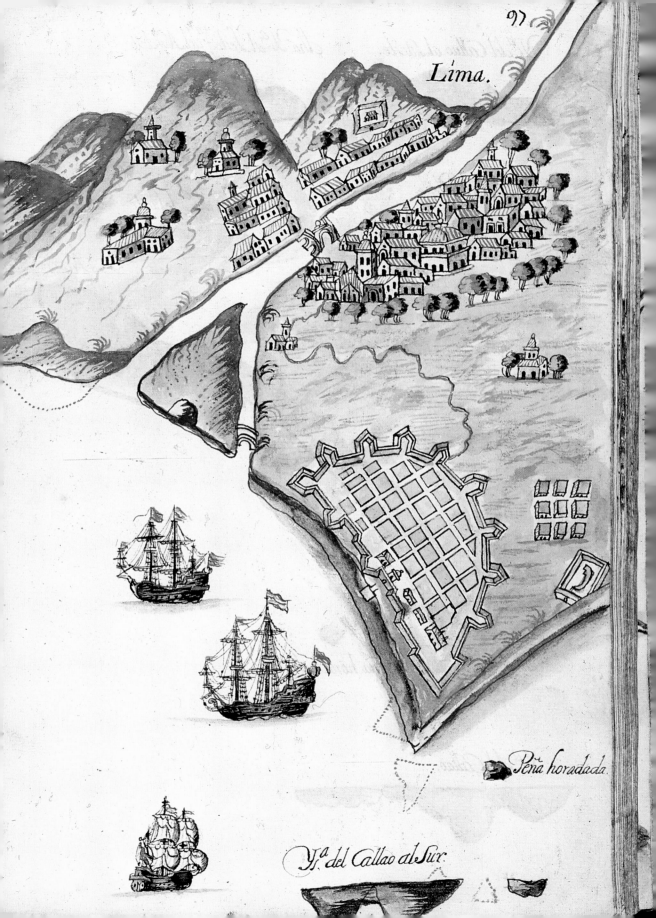

Lima.

Peña horadada.

Y.ª del Callao al Sur.

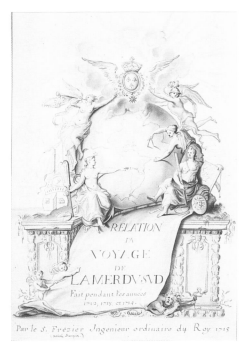

In the seventeenth century, the Dutch took over the exploration of the southern lands, starting with Java. They discovered the north of Australia, Tasmania, and New Zealand, although they did not manage to put all this information together in a coherent way. At the end of this century, Hollandia Nova was still only a hypothetical embryo of something that could perhaps be the *Terra Australis Incognita*. In 1722, a Dutch navigator, Jakob Roggeven, suggested that this land, if it existed, could not have a temperate climate and would instead be in the grips of a glacially cold climate. A French engineer by the name of Amédée Frézier had just put forward the same hesitations after spending some time in the area of Terra del Fuego, at the edge of the ice. No one paid any attention to their comments, especially as the existence of a large landmass—discovered south of the Indian Ocean in the early sixteenth century by Paulmier de Gonneville—was accepted as fact. We know today that the land he encountered was, in all probability, Brazil.

Several French expeditions were sent toward de Gonneville's land, in the exploratory tradition of the Indies trading companies. Jean-Baptiste Bouvet de Lozier received orders to search for a stopping point for the trading company's ships and to create and maintain a friendly and trusting relationship with the natives. At latitude 54° S, an inaccessible cape looming out of the fog seemed to indicate a sterile continent. "On the first of January 1739, around three o'clock in the afternoon, we saw a very high landmass, which was covered with snow and surrounded by fog. It looked to be a large headland, and we named it the Cape of Circumcision." Bouvet Island is one of the rare landmasses in the South Atlantic. Bouvet de Lozier was greatly disappointed, and on his return was treated as an incompetent navigator. The cartographer Philippe Buache listened to the sailors and in 1744 he drew up a map of the Antarctic Ocean which eliminated the utopian visions and portrayed the southern continent with its correct dimensions. He declared that New Holland (Australia) was the only inhabitable land in the south seas.

Paradoxically, Bouvet de Louzier's failure, which dampened sailors' enthusiasm and stopped exploratory voyages for thirty years, revived the enthusiastic imagination of partisans of the *Terra Australis Incognita*. They were supported by the *Encylopédie,* Buffon, President Charles de Brosses (a major figure in the field

Title page of the manuscript *Relation de Voyage de le Mer du Sud aux côtes du Chili et du Pérou en 1712, 1713, 1714* by Amédée Frézier (1715).

Right:
Ceremonial headdress from Vanuatu. Melanesia, situated between the Indonesian islands held by the Dutch in the seventeenth century, and the Pacific Islands, explored in the eighteenth century, was one of the last regions in the world to be discovered. It had been settled by the Maori during a mass migration over three thousand years ago. The Melanesian culture was one of the most savage: it practiced ritual cannibalism through the twentieth century, yet was also one of the most creative in the history of art.

of geography) and his Scottish analogue, the great Alexander Dalrymple. In 1752, Pierre-Louis de Maupertuis lent the full weight of his authority to this hypothesis, which he believed was an obvious fact: "Everyone knows that there is an unknown area in the southern hemisphere where there is a new part of the world, larger than any of the four others. The *Terra Australis Incognita*, beyond Africa, is much closer to the equator, and it stretches as far as the lands where the most valuable products of nature are found." A series of poorly prepared and catastrophic French voyages took place in the 1770's. The sum total of their discoveries in the polar environment of the enormous southern sea was Marion Island and the Crozet Islands—paid for heavily with the death of hundreds of sailors. Among the casualties were eighteen men, including ship captain Marc-Joseph Marion-Dufresne, who were massacred and eaten in New Zealand by the Maori. Jules-Marie Crozet (for whom the islands were named) wrote from Possession Island: "I was not able to discover on the island any tree or shrub whatsoever. This island, battered with the continuous force of the violent westerly winds that blow year round in the region, does not appear to be habitable."

THE DELUSSION OF AUSTRAL FRANCE

At this same time, Yves Joseph de Kerguelen-Trémarec, a naval officer and hydrographer, received approval from King Louis XV of France to pursue his proposed voyage to de Gonneville's land. "The discovery of the *Terra Australis* is one of the most important goals for navigation, increasing trade, and even the power of the State." His campaign was one of the most controversial and chaotic in the history of the discoveries.

"Lord de Kerguelen is hereby notified of the primary goal of his mission. The trust His Majesty has in [Kerguelen's] knowledge, talents, energy, and activity was instrumental in his decision to give him preference to undertake one of the most important discoveries that remains to be made. Lord de Kerguelen is instructed that, to all appearances, there exists a very large continent south of the Saint Paul and Amsterdam Islands, which must occupy a large part of the globe from latitude 45° S to the pole itself, in an immense area which has barely been penetrated. It appears fairly certain, however, that Lord de Gonneville landed there around the

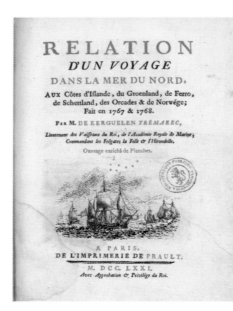

Title page for *Relation d'un voyage dans la mer du Nord* [...] *made in 1767 & 1768* [...] by Yves de Kerguelen-Trémarec (1771). Captain of the corvette *Folle,* then of the *Hirondelle.*

year 1504, and spent nearly six months there, during which he was extremely well treated by the people of this land. He shall set sail toward this land, leaving from the Île de France [Mauritius] with the corvette given to him for the purposes of this discovery voyage. He shall do everything in his power to find them and explore them. If he manages to discover them, he shall seek a port where he can find shelter. He shall take all necessary precautions to disembark safely. He shall try to forge trading and friendly relations with the inhabitants. He shall examine the products of the country, its culture, its goods, if there are any, and determine how the commerce of the realm could benefit from it."

The *Fortune* and the transport ship *Gros-Ventre* set sail from Île de France on January 16, 1772. "On February 10, we had hail and snow, we almost always had stormy weather, strong winds, and heavy seas from latitude 40° S onward." The two small boats sailed through the Roaring Forties, without even any warm clothes for the benumbed crew. "Above all, we were hindered by a fog that was so thick, it was impossible to make out an object no more than a gunshot's distance away; we spent nights, and even some days, hove to, when the thick fog joined forces with the violent winds." On February 12, a jagged coastline loomed out of the snow flurries and icy mists. Under extremely perilous conditions, an act signaling possession was placed on the island by the ship's lieutenant, du Boisguehenneuc. Then, as the two boats struggled to stay afloat, they lost sight of one another.

Despite the apocalyptic circumstances surrounding the discovery of this fragment of inhospitable land, Kerguelen returned to France, without a backward glance at his lost convoy, which he declared lost. He then confidently declared that this land did indeed seem to be the center of a fifth continent. "I called these lands France Septentrionnelle and their position gives them control of India, the Molucca Islands, China, and the southern seas. They shall provide harvests and wood; these lands shall prove to be as fertile as those in France." And he went on, in the inimitable style of the Enlightenment: "We shall perhaps find new men. If we do not find men

Title page for *Relation de deux voyages Dans les Mers Australes & aux Indes, made in 1771, 1772, 1773, and 1774 by M. de Kerguelen* (1782).

Sentenced in 1775 and imprisoned, then liberated by Louis XVI in 1778 (though not acquitted), he published his *Relation* in his own defense. The Convention reinstated him to his previous rank, and in 1793, he was promoted to rear-admiral.

of a different species, we shall at least find native peoples, living in a primitive state, without suspicion, without remorse, and ignorant of the artifices of civilized men."

The governor of Île de France, Chevalier des Roches, was no less enthusiastic in his letter to the Secretary of State for the Navy and the Colonies: "Your Lordship, M. de Kerguelen shall report back to you concerning the campaign he has just completed. He shall provide you with the most interesting details and I would not want to compromise his advantage by presenting them to you directly. But I would like to take this opportunity to have the honor of once again praising the superior talents of this officer. They have been confirmed by his unprecedented success, as he had been gone from this colony for sixty days, yet he successfully did what we requested and what [navigators] have been trying to achieve, in vain, for more then one hundred years." Lying on latitude 49° 30' S, the Kerguelen Islands are practically at the same latitude as Paris. As everyone seemed blind to the obvious climatic differences between the two hemispheres, he added, as though he were a victim of some contagious delusion: "If we consider the latitude of explored lands, we cannot prevent ourselves from attributing to this lands a gentle climate, pleasant temperatures, as well as extremely fertile soil—which naturally must parallel all of our needs. On the one hand, everything that they were able to see was covered with wood and greenery, which seems to mean this is an inhabited and well-planned cultivated country."

In March of 1772, during the exhausting return of the *Gros-Ventre,* Louis-François d'Alleno de Saint-Allouarn sailed alongside and mapped the west coast of New Holland, which was as yet virtually unexplored by the Dutch. The ship's log includes the following entries for May 30 and 31: "Hugged the coast, one and a half leagues away, along sandy beaches without any trees. As a reef runs along the coast, we kept starboard to the wind to move closer to land, and take depth soundings. Fine, muddy sand. We send our launch to the beach with two officers, who explored the land at noon. We saw large numbers of cormorants and sea swallows." Later: "Sand dunes covered with scrub and reeds. Many tortoises on the shores and gathered lots of eggs." He went on: "See lots of smoke." And in Shark

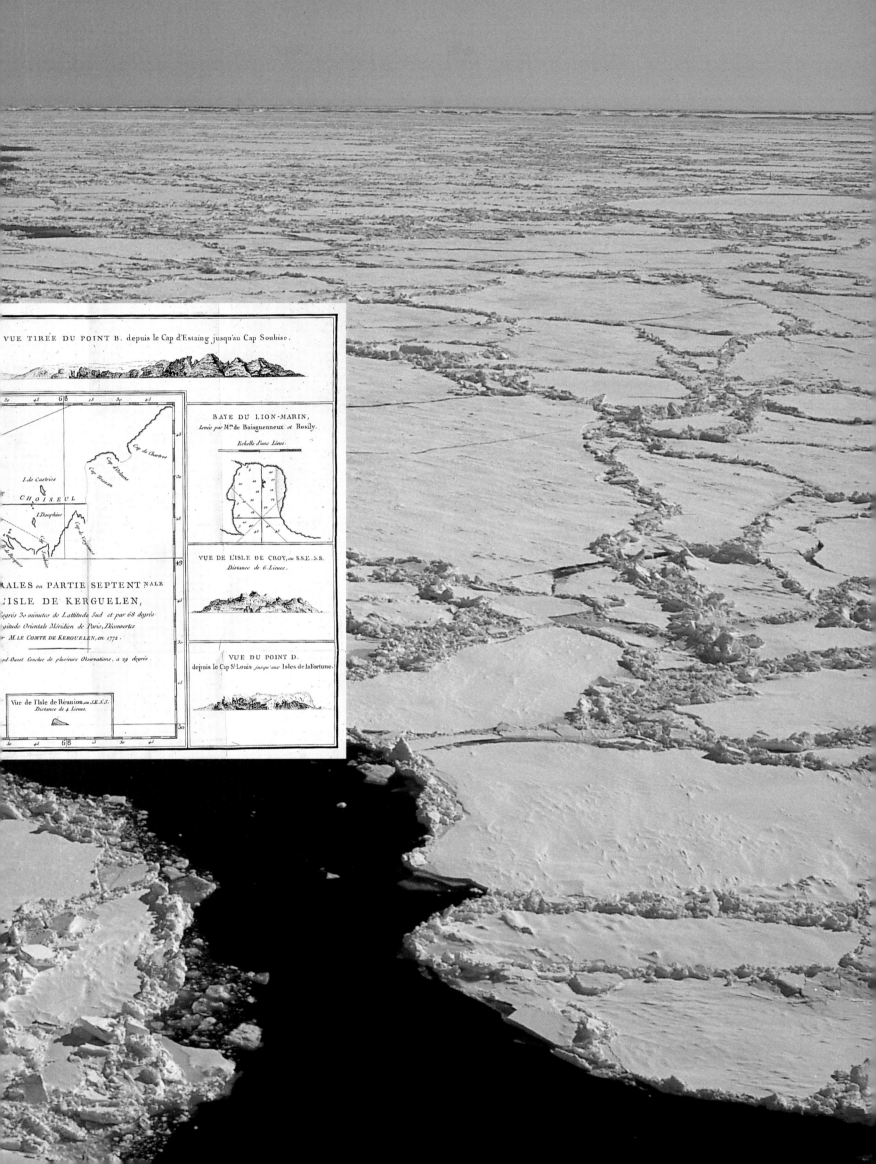

VUE TIRÉE DU POINT B. depuis le Cap d'Estaing jusqu'au Cap Soubise.

Cap de Chartres

Cap d'Orléans

I. de Castries

Cap Broyeur

CHOISEUL

I. Dauphine

Cap de Voyageurs

BAYE DU LION-MARIN,
Levée par Mrs. de Boisquenneux et Rosily.

Echelle d'une Lieue.

VUE DE L'ISLE DE CROY, ou S.S.E. 5.S.
Distance de 6 Lieues.

...RALES ou PARTIE SEPTENT.NALE
...'ISLE DE KERGUELEN,
...degrés 30 minutes de Lattitude Sud et par 68 degrés
...gitude Orientale Méridien de Paris, Découvertes
...M. LE COMTE DE KERGUELEN, en 1772.

...rd Ouest Conclue de plusieurs Observations, à 29 degrés.

VUE DU POINT D.
depuis le Cap St Louis jusqu'aux Isles de la Fortune.

Vue de l'Isle de Réunion, ou S.E.S.S.
Distance de 4 Lieues.

Bay: "We sent our boat to claim possession of the land in the name of France." Saint-Allouarn died in Île de France on October 27. France never claimed West Australia, but it kept the Kerguelen Islands.

Meanwhile, rumors were swirling around Kerguelen, partly because of jealously and partly because of suspicions concerning his conduct as commander in chief. He left Brest in May of 1773 for another voyage, with specific instructions: "To seek the most suitable place to start a settlement and start it, if he deems it to be so."

The delivery of the *Journal d'Amsterdam* on November 4, 1774 reported what happened next. "On January 9, with fairly good weather, we set sail at daybreak to anchor, but at 8 o'clock, a terrible storm struck: we had to run under bare poles. The ships were covered with snow, and several sailors aboard the *Roland* were so cold after stowing the sails that we had to use cords to get them down, as they were frozen and unconscious. At noon, the thermometer dropped to 2° above freezing. After this wind, we had several others, one after another. Finally, on January 18, M. de Kerguelen, seeing one hundred fifty sick men and the rest of his crew exhausted, called his officers in for counsel during which it was decided that the ship would sail to the nearest port. As a result, we set sail for Madagascar, where there were cattle and everything necessary for those suffering from scurvy. After one month, the crew had revived enough to put out to sea and sail to the Cape; we put into port to replenish our supplies, and on June 26, M. de Kerguelen set sail to return to France, which he reached on September 7."

As he rounded the Cape of Good Hope, Kerguelen, sick at heart, wrote to the Secretary of State for the Navy and Colonies: "The *Terra Australis* that we explored seems to have no resources. They are covered almost entirely with snow: all we saw on land were seals, penguins, and other sea birds. There are no signs that the

country is inhabited, at least we saw nothing that would indicate so, and the cold weather we experienced along with the continuous storms do not inspire us to think so." There was nothing left to protect Kerguelen from a court martial. Even more important than the charges against him was the fact that he had torpedoed the idea of an Austral France. He was sentenced to six years' imprisonment.

During James Cook's second voyage, he pushed the *HMS Adventure* and *HMS Resolution* (three times in 1773) beyond the Antarctic polar circle, reaching a field of ice that stretched as far as the eye could see. On January 30, he sailed to a record latitude of 71° 11' S. His log entry put a definitive end to the controversy: "I cannot say that it was absolutely impossible to continue southward, but the attempt was arduous and perilous, and in my opinion, no navigator would have dreamed of it. My opinion, and that of most of the officers, is that this ice stretches to the pole or to some other land and has been here since ancient times... As we approached this ice, we could hear the cries of penguins, but we could not see them. We only observed a few birds, which could have indicated the proximity of land. Yet I believe that a land must exist farther to the south of this ice barrier, but if it exists, it can offer birds and other animals no more shelter that the ice itself, with which it is, to all appearances, entirely covered... I do not deny that there exists a continent or vast stretch of land near the pole; on the contrary, it is my opinion that there is one: and it is probable that we have explored a part of it."

THE DISCOVERY OF CAPE HORN: A USELESS EXPLOIT

Cape Horn was rounded for the first time on January 29, 1616 by Jakob Le Maire, son of a Huguenot refugee in Antwerp, and Willem Cornelisz Schouten. One of the logs, written by Aris Claes, offers a sober account of the discovery of what was merely, in the minds of the financial backers, a way of bypassing the privilege granted to the Dutch East Indies trading company, the VOC. Its store ships were the only boats authorized to either cross the meridian of the Cape of Good Hope heading east, or to go through the Strait of Magellan westward, on their way to the Pacific.

The *Eendracht* and the store ship *Hoorn* were commissioned by the Austral

Company founded by two families and several shareholders. They set sail from the small town of Hoorn, on the Zuiderdee on May 25, 1615, in search of several landmasses: Magallinica, the southern lands depicted on world maps drawn by their friend, the cartographer Petrus Plancius; the Solomon Islands; and the land of Ophir that the Spanish

134

THE BOOK
OF
DISILLUSIONMENT

Right:
Indigenous peoples in the
Strait of Magellan.
"Immediately, the women
dove into five or six
fathoms, naked as the day,
with admirable skill...
They dove with one leg
crossed over the other with
such skill that, although
they were totally naked,
it was impossible to see that
which modesty has us
conceal." September 1699.
Manuscript log by
Duplessis, Beauchesne's
cartographer and engineer
aboard the *Maurepas*.

Following double page:
The Eendracht *Leaving
the Ijssel.* June 14, 1615.
Painting by Aert Anthonisz,
1618.

had been seeking for nearly a half a century. They also, of course, intended to reach
the Molucca Islands.

They followed Magellan's route. The *Hoorn* burned accidentally in Patagonia
during makeshift repairs. Everyone crowded aboard the *Eendracht,* which continued
to head south toward the end of the world. "On the 29th at night, we once again
caught a glimpse of the land to the NW and NNW. This was the country south of
the Strait of Magellan, high, mountainous, and covered with snow; it ended to the
south at latitude 57° 48' S, at a headland we called Cape Horn. The weather was
fair, but in the evening, the wind turned to the north; we continued our route
westward, where we encountered extremely heavy seas. On the 30th, we still had
heavy rollers from the west and the sea was still blue. Taking together, these signs
gave us confidence and supported our belief that we had found a new route leading
to the Great South Sea... The persistence of the strong, blue-colored swells
confirmed our suspicion that no land lay before us, only an immense sea."

Several days later, a heavy snowstorm struck; it was so violent and so cold that
they had to shorten the sails, then "let the ship float under bare poles, at the mercy
of the wind and waves... On February 12, each man received a triple ration of wine

in celebration of our triumph: we had indeed achieved our goal, having discovered and gone through a new passage." Ever since, the branch of the sea between the Tierra del Fuego and Los Estados Island has been called the Strait of Le Maire.

Ten months later, the ship was seized by the governor of Jakarta, which would become Batavia, capital of the Dutch East Indies, and the crew was sent back to Holland. The Austral trading company was perfectly within its rights, but the privileges of the VOC were so entrenched that the embarrassing lawsuit lasted twenty-five years. An unexpected consequence of this useless exploit was that a small, unknown port of Zuiderdee, Hoorn, would lend its name to the most famous headland on earth.

Guy Bernardin, a contemporary solitary navigator, reported in his log how, on a brilliantly clear night, he started up a radio communication with a cargo ship whose lights appeared intermittently in the huge swells of Cape Horn. His traveling companion had only a single phrase for the sailor: *"Yo tengo sueño,"* ("I'm sleepy"). As he was rounding this legendary cape, all he experienced was supreme fatigue. He was expressing the sentiment of millions of unknown sailors, forgotten by history, as he pursued the banal and marvelous destiny of the seafaring man.

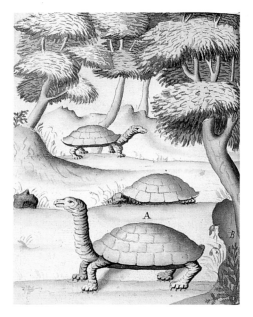

Preceding double page:
A Chief of the Sandwich Islands (detail) by John Webber, painter and illustrator aboard Cook's third voyage, 1787.

Left:
Roteiro (chart) by Francisco de Roís, pilot for António de Miranda Azevedo's fleet, who created a Portuguese settlement on the Moluccas in 1513-1516.

Below right:
Moluccan women with cloves. The clove tree (*Eugenia aromatica*) grew only on a handful of small islands, the most famous of which were the twin volcanic islands Tidore and Ternate, in the Molucca Islands.
Géographie du Monde by Artus Fonnant, 1633.

The exploration of the world revealed the presence of people called "savages"—a designation that mirrored the contrasts, in Europe, between well-kept, planned parks, gardens, and cultivated fields and untamed "wild" nature, left to grow free.

The encounter between the special envoys from the Western world and these unknown people—whose cultures, religions, rites, and rituals were measured against the standards of European society—created a great many misconceptions. Conversely, these Europeans, in their odd get-ups, appeared to be puny and weak, despite their terrifying weapons; they were probably viewed with more perplexity than fear by the indigenous people. Although these encounters were often pleasant, the consequences of the incomprehension between two different worlds were sometimes catastrophic.

The Moluccas are a group of a thousand islands that straddle the equator over a large area stretching from the Banda Sea between Borneo and the Celebes to the west, and New Guinea to the east. These islands, the historic Spice Islands, are the tips of volcanoes that have risen from the ocean floor; they offered abundant supplies of the goods coveted by the Renaissance discoverers. Yet the black pearls, gathered by divers from Aru Island in shark-infested waters, cassowary and bird of paradise feathers, and fabulous butterflies were almost insignificant when compared to the fabulous natural beauty of these sites. The Banda Islands in the south had the unique privilege of harboring a seemingly innocuous shrub, *Myristica fragrans*, which grew around the still-active volcano Gunung Api. The rich volcanic soil, combined with a tropical climate, offered ideal conditions for the nutmeg plant; indeed these islands were the only place on Earth where the spice grew. Yet there was more. Ternate, Tidore, Motir, Makian, and Bacan, small islands off the coast of Halmahera, the largest of the Moluccas, were the exclusive habitat of *Eugenia aromatica,* or clove tree, which grew on the slopes of Gunung Gamalama and Gunung Kiematubu.

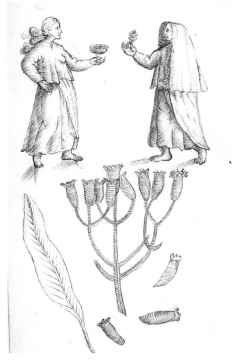

The history of spices can be traced to the complex routes taken by ocean-going caravels and the crusaders, as well as to superstitions and fashions. Man has used scents and fragrances to communicate with the gods since the dawn of time. Spices offered a bulwark against the illnesses and epidemics that lurked in crowded, unhealthy cities.

Bland or decaying food was also improved by spices, which had been in widespread use since ancient Roman times. The potential profits in the spice trade were enormous. The noble Portuguese undertaking to the Indies may have been motivated, at least publicly, by religious fervor to convert the heathens, yet reaching the source of the spice trade would guarantee that the extravagant costs of the slow and difficult circumnavigation of Africa was covered.

Columbus stumbled across something—an outlying region of Asia or an unknown continent—but it clearly had nothing to do with the Spice Islands. Even before they were discovered, it was unclear which country, Portugal or Spain, could lay claim to the territory. The Treaty of Tordesillas divided the world between the two kingdoms, with the benediction of the Pope. This demarcation was already fairly undefined in the Atlantic, but the situation was far worse in the southern seas. No one yet knew the precise circumference of the Earth, and no one had yet explored the undefined region that separated the China that Marco Polo described and the China that Christopher Columbus seems to have reached. The existing information seemed to point to the fact that, making due allowance for the geographical approximations of this time, the Moluccas were situated more or less on the

eastern boundary line of the treaty. Given that the unforeseen landmass of the Americas formed an impenetrable north to south barrier, blocking the most direct passage to the Indies, Ferdinand Magellan proposed circumnavigating it to the south, via routes known to this sailor alone.

AROUND THE WORLD TO THE MOLUCCAS

Ferdinand Magellan grew up at a time when the future looked brighter than ever for a young, ambitious man who could earn honor and duties in the Indies. Born into a proud though poor noble Portuguese family, Magellan was an awkward, arrogant court follower. He was not able to obtain from King Manuel of Portugal the rewards he felt he deserved, and decided to offer his services to Spain. As a foreigner in this neighboring country, he knew no one and had to struggle for recognition. Spain had been bogged down in its efforts to reach the East for nearly twenty-five years. Spanish navigators had not yet set foot in either Mexico or Peru, and were unaware of the Eldorado they would soon discover. Advisors to Emperor Charles V agreed to grant this turncoat command of an expedition, which was given instruction to reach the Moluccas by circumnavigating the New World to the south. Magellan's ship log was kept by Antonio Pigafetta from Vicenza, a subaltern officer under the commander's orders—and fortunately, one of the eighteen survivors who limped into Seville in 1522.

The fleet set sail on September 20, 1519, from Sanlúcar de Barrameda. The long trip past Patagonia as the winter approached was difficult. The sailors considered the St. Elmo's fire they saw along the route as a luminous message of hope. "One very dark night, in bad weather, Saint Anselm appeared in the form of a fire burning on top of the mainmast, where he remained for more than two and a half hours, which comforted all of us, as we were all shedding tears, waiting only for the moment we would perish. And when this sainted light decided to leave us, it had been so bright that we were blinded for one quarter of an hour, begging for mercy, for no one believed we would escape from the storm." Today, few people see anything mystical in this bluish glow, a meteorological phenomenon caused by the ionization process that occurs during storms.

The Spanish captains and other dignitaries holding royal offices were soon bristling under the authority of this foreigner of lesser nobility. Tensions rose and a rebellion broke out on Easter Monday, while the ships were at anchor in a sinister bay that Magellan had chosen for winter quarters. The rebellion was instantly and ruthlessly crushed; the mutineers were decapitated, and the bodies quartered with

Left:
Portrait of Magellan.
Anonymous, undated.

Map of Tierra del Fuego
and the Strait of Magellan.
Drawing by Lord Labat,
aboard the *Phélypeaux*.
Log from Beauchesne's
voyage (1698-1701).

Background image:
Symbolic portrait of
Magellan holding a pair of
dividers used to transfer
points to nautical charts.
*Les vrais Portraits et Vies des
Hommes illustres*. André
Thévet, 1584.

Following double page:
*Rio da Prata, Estreito do
Magalhais*. This 16th-
century Spanish map
includes the southern tip
of America, from the
Rio da Prata to the Strait
of Magellan.
On this chart, Tierra del
Fuego is still indicated
as the beginning of a
southern continent.

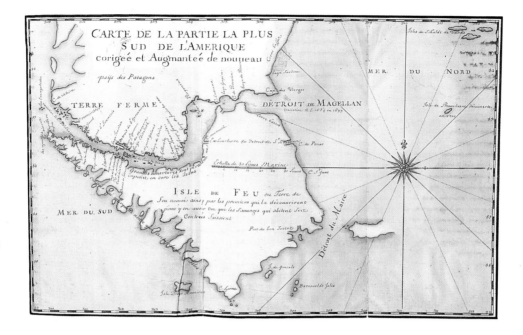

the help of the *Trinidad's* capstan. Juan de Cartagena, the king's representative, was abandoned to divine mercy, along with a traitorous priest.

On October 21, 1520, one year after leaving Seville, Magellan sailed past a headland at the entrance to an immense stretch of sea and named it the Cape of Eleven Thousand Virgins, in honor of Saint Ursula. Two ships were sent to reconnoiter, despite the foul weather. "Between us, we believed they had perished, first of all because of the great storm, and also because we had not seen them for two days. As worried as we were, we saw the two ships in full sail, with flags flying, heading straight toward us. When they were near our ships, they fired all their artillery; in response, we joyfully saluted them with artillery and shouts. After, we all thanked God and the Virgin Mary and sailed on ahead."

On November 28, the three remaining ships (out of five that had sailed from Seville) entered the new ocean, which they named the Pacific, as the weather was calm and sunny. Yet the hardest part still lay ahead. "We made good headway through the aforesaid strait, and we entered into the Pacific Ocean, where we remained for three months and twenty days, without any fresh food or drink. All we had to eat was old hardtack, which had turned into powder and was full of worms and stank of rats that had defecated there once they had eaten what was still good. We drank stinking yellow water. We also ate the leather that had been wrapped around the main yard to keep the ropes from rubbing against each other and snapping. They were hardened by the sun, rain, and wind. We soaked them in seawater for four or five days, then put them over the coals for a while, and then ate them. And we also ate a lot of sawdust, and rats, which each cost a *demi-écu*— and even so, we couldn't catch enough of them." This account is not an exaggeration, as these conditions were not unusual during ocean-going

RITO·· QVE·ESTA·EM·S4

RAR·POR·ESTE·

ES TREITO

MALVCO

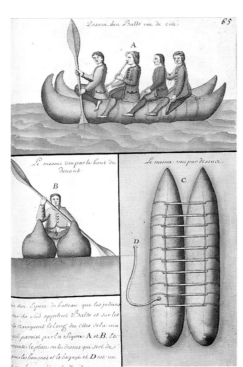

expagellis. Two centuries later, Bougainville would offer some already well-known words of advice: "It must also be forbidden to eat the leather wrapped around the yards, and the other old leathers; this food can cause fatal indigestion."

Worse still was scurvy, caused by a vitamin C deficiency. Symptoms began to appear among the sailors on board Magellan's ships after about two months without fresh food. "Most of the teeth of our men were so twisted, both above and below, that they couldn't even eat and died from this." Nineteen men perished of this illness, which weakens the walls of blood vessels, resulting in bleeding. Scurvy plagued the crews of ocean-going vessels throughout the nineteenth century. A sailing mate of Charles Fleury, a seventeenth-century buccaneer, provided his description of the disease: "Your mouth hurts so much that it produces large chunks of rotten flesh, causing great swelling and putrefaction; they have to be cut out with a razor and all that can be eaten is very liquid food. Besides this, teeth become so loose that they can be pulled out easily without pain, and this skin must continually be cut."

Five months after entering the Pacific Ocean, Magellan received a fatal wound on Mactan in the Philippines, as he stood up to Cilapulapu, a vassal of King Cebu, who refused to pay allegiance to the king of Spain; he sent a group of one thousand savage warriors against the organized forces of Charles V's soldiers—some fifty soldiers. The battle was over before it even began.

Under assault by the natives and wounded in the leg and head, Magellan fell and was murdered by a wrathful hoard. He died, a victim of his own memories of battles in the Indies, and especially of unfounded confidence in the superior power of his weapons.

Eighteen survivors of the two hundred who set sail on the first expedition to sail around the world returned to Seville in 1522, after three years at sea and a voyage of some 53,000 miles. Everyone had long since given up hope of ever seeing the battered *Victoria* again. Charles V gave Juan Sebastián del Cano a hero's welcome.

The *Trinidad* had failed in its attempt to sail against the winds to return across the Pacific, and the survivors of this agonizing trip

Small boat from Gouane Island off the coast of Peru, described by Duplessis in these words: "Made of two sacks of goat's skin sewn together with pointed ends. These sacks could be inflated like balloons… Strips of wood connected with straps meant that these boats could carry four or five men; the one in front propelled the boat with a large oar."
Manuscript journal by Duplessis, engineer and cartographer with Beauchesne aboard the *Maurepas* (1698-1701).

Sea lion in the Strait of Magellan.

The harquebusiers and the crossbowmen shot in vain from a long distance, for nearly thirty minutes, managing only to pierce their targes [shields] made of old planks and braces... When they saw that we were shooting our harquebuses in vain, they shouted and understood that they were still strong. Yet they shouted even louder when we fired the harquebuses and then they were not immobilized by fear, but jumped all around, shileding themselves with their targes. Defending themselves in this way, they shot so many arrows, spears, pointed burned stakes, and stones that we could barely defend ourselves... Our large artillery pieces on the ships could not help us as their range was too far.

Antonio de Pigafetta, *Navigation et descouvrement de la Indie supérieure faicte par moy Anthoyne Pigaphete Vincente Chevallier de Rhodes,*
Magellan's travel log, 1519-1522.
Pigafetta was one of the eighteen survivors of Magellan's two hundred thirty-seven original crew members.

were imprisoned on the Moluccas by the Portuguese. Four men, more dead than alive, were one day returned to Charles V. It is said that the Casa de Contratación, which managed the affairs of the Indies, deducted from their pay the time they spent interned in Portuguese prisons. Del Cano died at sea, aboard the fleet that set sail in 1525 to repeat their first journey. He had just replaced the commander, who had died several days earlier. Like dozens of his shipmates, victims of illness and accidents, he was buried at sea, somewhere in the Pacific Ocean.

Magellan had an advantage over other sailors in his attempt to sail around the world, as he had already spent years sailing in the East as far as Malacca. Yet, in a fluke of history, he was not the first man to accomplish this feat. One month before his death, while the ships were exploring a small Philippine island, "a slave belonging to the commander, a native of Sumatra, in other words Taprobane, spoke to people in the distance in their own language, and they approached the ship." Magellan had purchased this slave at the Malacca market many years earlier, when he was serving in the Indies as a young officer. He renamed him Henrique, the name of that day's saint, and brought him back to Lisbon. As Henrique was born somewhere east of Malacca, and had started his long journey at a point farther east than that of Magellan and his companions, he was, in fact, the first man to have actually sailed fully around the world.

The question of who owned the Moluccas remained controversial for many years. The Treaty of Saragossa in 1529 confirmed the existing situation, attributing the Philippines to Spain and the Moluccas to Portugal. Starting in 1565, when the first successful west-to-east crossing of the Pacific was made, Spain could pursue trade with the Philippines via Mexico. The favorable west winds, which the *Trinidad* could not find, blow most strongly at latitudes near Japan. The Manila galleons then set out from Acapulco, braving the perils of the sea, reefs, illness, pirates, and European raiders to make the 10,000-mile crossing, one of the most prestigious sea trading routes in history. Heading west, the trip usually took three months, sometimes as long as five; the return voyage lasted six months.

NEW CYTHEREA

English explorers began to sail the Pacific during the latter half of the sixteenth century, encouraged by Queen Elizabeth to pillage Spanish settlements in the New World. Francis Drake and Thomas Cavendish, who were fearsome figures on the high seas, also sailed around the world. One century later, William Dampier, then George Anson, set sail for the Pacific.

In the middle of the eighteenth century, advances in the fields of science and philosophy began to have an influence on the spirit of exploratory voyages, although imperialist designs

Right:
View of ships heading toward the coast and map of the Bay of Nombra di Deos. This was a major Spanish embarcation site for precious metals from Peru, along with Porto Bello, where Francis Drake died of dysentery a few days later.
Drawing with watercolor. Page from Francis Drake's last log (1595-1596).

Below:
Sir Francis Drake. Portrait by Isaac Oliver (1565-1617).

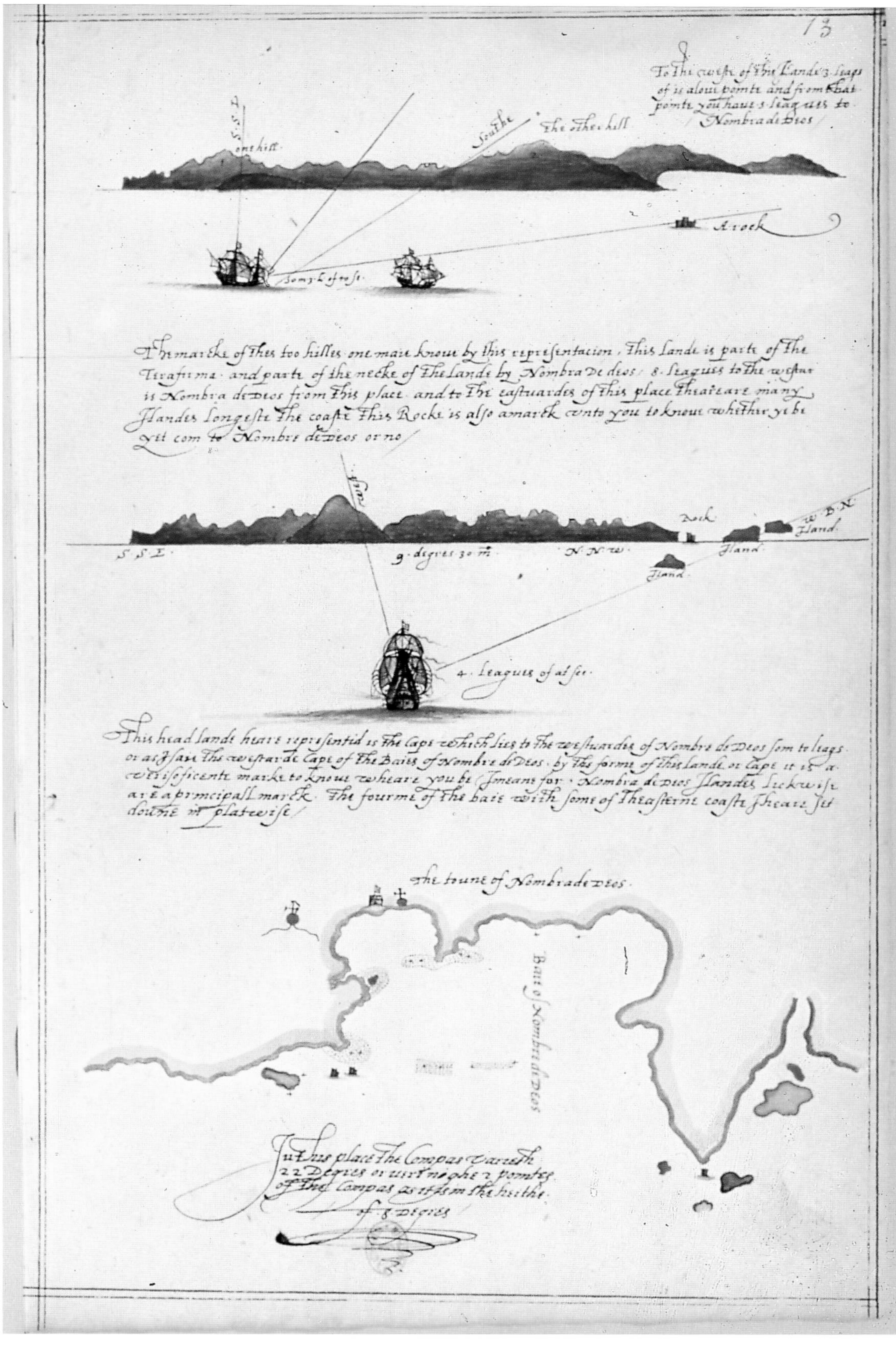
A rock
Thmarcke of thes too hilles one maie knowe by this representacion, This lande is parte of the Tirafirma and parte of the necke of the lande by Nombra de deos, 8 leagues to the westuar is Nombra de deos from this place and to the eastuardes of this place theare are many Ilandes longeste the coaste This Rocke is also amarck unto you to knowe whether ye be yet com to Nombre de deos or no
Rock
Iland
4 leagues of at see
This head lande heare representid is the cape which lies to the westuardes of Nombre de Deos som 10 leags or as I saie the westuarde cape of the Baies of Nombre de Deos by the forme of this lande or cape it is a verrie soficente marke to knowe wheare you be I meane for Nombra de Deos Ilandes lickewise are a principall marck The fourme of the baie with some of the asterne coaste I heare set downe in platewise
The toune of Nombra de Deos

still carried weight. Ambitious naval expeditions between 1768 and 1794 nearly completed exploration of the Pacific, from the Bering Strait to the Antarctic. Naval expeditions provided scholarly annals with a vast body of knowledge during the last third of the eighteenth century, on the same scale with Linneaus's and Georges de Buffon's theories on natural history; President Charles de Brosses' and Alexander Dalrymple's theories on geography; Diderot and d'Alembert's *Encyclopedia,* and the *Encyclopedia Brittanica.*

America gradually began to expel France and England from its soil, taking its fate in its own hands. As a result, France and England became rivals for control of the Pacific. The Pacific had been a source of great disappointment, having fueled the hopes and desires over the mythical *Terra Australis Incognita.* The idea of economic windfalls and overseas trading centers were part of overall scientific motives for exploration. France and England alone backed international efforts to explore the Pacific, understand hydrography and the Earth's magnetism and climate, identify species, and inventory various cultures and peoples for nearly half a century. Beyond scientific observations, the voyages provided an opportunity for on-site verification of Buffon's, Voltaire's, and Rousseau's ideas and philosophies.

To start, there was the entire Pacific region, inhabited by people who were friendly and trusting at times, and hostile and crude at others, and its enchanting landscape. Then there was Tahiti, the pearl and exception, an anomaly of nature, paradise on Earth, "the enchanted island of Calypso." Those writing about its wonders showed a bit of restraint, so as not to be seen as immoral.

After Commodore John Byron's fruitless voyage in pursuit of unexplored territory, Samuel Wallis set sail from Plymouth in 1766 for the Pacific. On June 19, 1767, he dropped anchor in Tahiti. At first, Wallis was wary, for the Maoris had treated them with great hostility, branding them intruders, before making peace. The Englishman responded to Queen Oberea's overtures, but he was more concerned with trading nails for a maximum number of black pigs, and to avoid the *Dolphin's* being dismantled by the crew, who was distributing nails to the women. "The only remaining means I had to prevent the total destruction of the

The *Dolphin* by Samuel Wallis, under attack by natives from the island of King George (Tahiti), June 1767. Anonymous watercolor by a member of Wallis's crew.

vessel and the rise in value of commodities to rates which we could have no longer afforded, was to forbid everyone from going ashore." He took possession of the island and dedicated it to King George III in a highly official ceremony before departing, leaving Queen Oberea and her subjects in tears. He was convinced that Tahitian society was extremely venal.

Louis Antoine de Bougainville. Portrait by Jean-Pierre Franquel (1774-1860).

Less than a year later, on April 6, 1768, the *Boudeuse* and the *Étoile* anchored at Hitiaa on the eastern coast of Tahiti, and the magic of the blissful islands was striking. Louis Antoine de Bougainville had just surrendered the Falkland Islands to Spain; he had tried to establish an Acadian colony here after the loss of Canada. He had been given orders to pursue his voyage and to take the first French Pacific expedition around the world.

A top scientist who loved high society and sophisticated literary culture, Bougainville instantly fell in love with a land in the midst of its golden age, living proof of the goodness of native customs, and powerful evidence of the easygoing way of life in the austral land. "The number of pirogues was so great around the ships, that we had a great deal of difficulty mooring in the midst of the crowd and the noise. They came towards us shouting Tayo, meaning friend, and offering us thousands of tokens of friendship. They all were asking for nails and earrings. The pirogues were filled with women who were as lovely and seductive as most of the women in Europe, for the beauty of their faces and their silhouette. A great number of these nymphs were naked... I wonder: how can some four hundred Frenchmen, young, strapping sailors, keep their minds on their work amidst such a spectacle, particularly as they have not seen women for over six months. Regardless of all the precautions taken, a young girl came aboard. She went to the quarter-deck and stood near one of the hatchways above the windlass; the hatchway was open as ventilation for those in the vicinity. The young girl carelessly let the loincloth she was draped in fall to the ground, and she appeared to all like Venus before the Phrygian shepherd: she was nearly celestial in form."

Jeanne Barré, a sturdy young woman from Burgundy, had disguised herself as a boy and passed herself off as the valet of

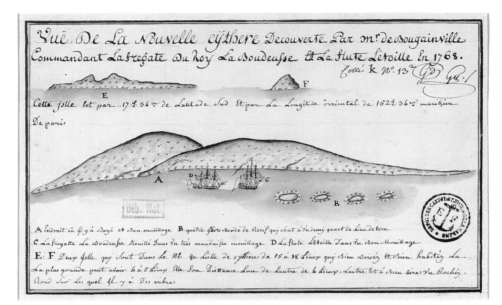

the naturalist Philibert Commerson. No one noticed, given the sheer number of ships, despite a few bawdy comments. Yet when they arrived in Tahiti, the first woman to sail around the world was quickly unmasked by the Tahitians, who knew she was a woman despite her disguise, and shouted out *"Vahiné! Vahiné!"* (woman). The brief nine-day stopover was typical of the frenzied schedule of the French navigators, who spent day after day out at sea in conditions propitious for falling victim to scurvy, leaving precious little time to the natives whose remarkable harvests were even more notable. Bougainville departed, bringing the young Aoturu with him, after taking possession of Tahiti on April 12. "This people exudes only rest and the pleasure of the senses. Venus is the goddess who is worshipped here. The mildness of the climate, the beauty of the landscape, the fertility of the soil everywhere irrigated by rivers and waterfalls, and the purity of the air inspires a great sense of voluptuousness. I therefore name the place New Cytherea, and Minerva's shield is as much a required part of life here as it was in Ancient times as protection against the influence of the climate and customs of the nation."

Although he acknowledged that the Tahitians were cruel warriors and unmitigated thieves (he was still unaware that human sacrifices were practiced ritually, which Cook discovered during his third stopover), Bougainville was inexhaustible. "The nation's character seemed to us to be gentle and benevolent. It does not seem that any kind of civil war exists on the island, nor any specific hatred. It is likely that the Tahitians demonstrate good faith amongst themselves and see this as inviolable… The air they breathe, the singing, the dancing are an undying reminder of the pleasures of love, there is such a movement for release. This custom of living life continuously in pleasure gives the Tahitians a marked predisposition for this sweet pleasantry, the daughter of rest and joy. There is also a certain lightness of heart in their character, which surprised us day after day.

Left:
Pirogue traveling by night.
Drawing with watercolor.
Maximilien Radiguet's
album.

Background image:
*Massacre of Sirs Langle,
Lamanon, and ten other
individuals from two
crews* in Manoua (Tutuila,
Samoa), December 1787.
Twelve members of two
crews, including Paul-
Antoine Fleuriot de Langle,
commander of the
Astrolabe, and the naturalist
Lamanon perished in a
watering place.
Drawing by Nicolas
Ozanne. Lapérouse's
voyage.

Right:
James Cook. Portrait by
Nathaniel Dance, 1776.

Whatever ill befalls them, they are not bothered." And this: "The chief offered me one of his young and rather fair wives, and the entire assembly sang the hymeneal. What a land, what a people!"

He left Tahiti exhibiting all the symptoms of a perfect utopist. "I could not fathom leaving this blissful island without renewing the praise which I have previously voiced. Nature has placed it within the most beautiful climate in the universe, embellished with the most pleasant aspects, rich with gifts and talents galore, filled with inhabitants that are beautiful, tall, and strong. She herself has dictated the laws; they abide by them peacefully and constitute what is perhaps the most blissful society that exists on this globe. Legislators and philosophers, come hither to see what your imagination could not even have dreamed. A well-populated civilization composed of handsome men and lovely women, living together in abundance and health, with all the signs of the greatest union... Having elementary knowledge in the arts sufficient for man living so close to nature, working little, reveling in all the pleasures of society, dance, music, conversation, love—the only god to whom these people sacrifice... To fully describe what we have seen, we would need Fénélon's feather-pen, to paint it would require the charming brush of Albane or Boucher."

After spending fine days in Parisian society, which soon grew weary of his inability to learn French, Aoturu was sent back to his island after a year's time. He died of measles en route, contracted on the Île de France (Mauritius).

Captain James Cook spent three months on the island of King George in 1769. Cook, who had charted the transit of Venus, was a rigorous professional intransigent in matters of discipline, hygiene, and cleanliness, and a great innovator in many fields. Without being overly puritanical, Cook stoically resisted the Tahitian women's charm. He managed to maintain a sense of discipline among the crew of the *Endeavour,* while granting a wide degree of freedom. His concern was to limit the spread of venereal disease. The naturalist Joseph Banks, who had easily seduced Queen Oberea in private, was subtly lyrical when he wrote that "the bodies

Left:
HMS Resolution. A ship
from Cook's second voyage
(1772-1775).
Watercolor by Henry
Roberts. He was fifteen
years old when he began
working as an apprentice
aboard the *Resolution.*

Right:
A double canoe from Tahiti.
Drawing with watercolor by
John Webber, an illustrator
and painter from the third
voyage (1776-1780),
August-December 1777.

Following double page:
Women from the Marquesa
Islands, 1842. The arrival
of English missionaries to
Tahiti in 1797 quickly
had an impact on Polynesian
education, mores and
customs, and attire.
Radiguet was bewitched:
"The attitudes and gestures
were so harmonious,
so graceful and elegant,
that even an artist with
the most refined taste would
have been delighted.
Some of the women were
draped in large swaths
of white cloth, most naked
to the waist, revealing
their pale copper-colored
skin. All of them wear
crowns of foliage and
flowers, and all of them
have thick grassy necklaces
that smell sweet."
Drawing with watercolor.
Maximilien Radiguet's
album, 1842.

and souls of women are fashioned to the nth degree of perfection." Cook was not captivated by the island of King George, to which he returned three times to the glee of his crew. His judgements on the people remained cold: "One could say about these people that they have escaped the curse that struck our fathers, and that they barely earn their daily bread by the sweat on their brow, the goodness of nature absolved them not only of the necessary, but also, in great abundance, of the superfluous." He appreciated their extreme cleanliness, despite their bad habit of smearing monoi all over themselves and of not hiding their refuse; and he cast a reproachful eye on their license, indecency, and liberty "unworthy of mankind and contrary to the fundamental principles of human nature." He came back to the question so that it would be clear once and for all, in terms which would have raised the indignation of Bougainville's companions. "A great injustice has been committed toward the women of Tahiti and the Society Islands by those who have depicted them, without exception, as being ready to grant their last wishes to whomever is willing to pay the price. But this is not the case." Next came a somewhat muddled explanation about a form of prostitution tolerated by Tahitian society, with an unexpected conclusion: "On the whole, any foreigner visiting England could, with the same amount of equity, paint a portrait of women there based on those who frequent ships in one of our seaports, or around Covent Garden." Comparing the art de vivre in New Cytherea to the baseness of the brothels of Liverpool or Plymouth was a somewhat audacious to do.

One of the naturalists who accompanied him on his second voyage, Johann Reinhold Forster, a German who had translated Bougainville, depicted the life of the Tahitians in more bucolic overtones. "One finds in the life of the islanders a constant level of happiness: they get up with the sun, go to wash in the river or the fountain, spend mornings working or taking walks, until the heat of the day

P. Max: Rad.

Top left:
Melanesian figures.
Drawing with watercolor.
Maximilien Radiguet's
album, 1842.

Top right:
Lotété, king of the
Marquesa Islands in 1842
during the declaration of
the protectorate. Radiguet
described his attire: "It was
attire in Louis XV style, in
red velveteen and trimmed
along the seams, with a
large pair of epaulettes. A
crown of gilded cardboard
spruced up by encrusted
glass and painted feathers
covered his head and
highlighted his blue face."
Drawing with watercolor.
Maximilien Radiguet's
album.

Bottom:
Ritual offering of a piglet to
Cook by the natives of the
Sandwich Islands (Hawaii),
January 1779. "He was
carrying a piece of red
material, which he wrapped
around Captain Cook's
shoulders, after which he
gave a piglet as a gift,
according to custom."
(Diary of Captain James
King.) Cook was
assassinated three weeks
later.
Engraving by Samuel
Middiman and John Hall
(1784) after an ink wash by
John Webber (1769).

Top right:
Drawing with watercolor.
Maximilien Radiguet's
album.

Following double page:
*Death of Cook in Kealakeku
Bay in Owhyhee* (Hawaii),
February 14, 1779. "He was
stabbed from behind, and
fell facedown into the sea."
(James King diary.)
Painting by George Carter
(1781).

begins to rise. They then retire to their dwellings, or rest in the shade of a tree. They smooth their hair, scenting it with fragrant oil, or they play the flute and sing, or listen to the warbling of the birds. At noon, they eat. After their meal, they continue their domestic pastimes, and one notices during this interval a kind of mutual affection that prevails in all hearts. We so delighted in this display of innocence and bliss. Gay outbursts without any evil intention, simple tales, joyful dancing, and a frugal supper brings us to evening: they wash a second time in the river, and thus conclude the day without worry or pain."

Everything summed up, Cook judged that "despite the benefits that nature has so generously granted them, (the island) produces nothing of great value in and of itself, or that is liable to be used for trading, so that the interest of its discovery lies through and through in the provisioning of ships crossing these seas."

The island of King George versus New Cytherea: did England deserve Tahiti? Rear-Admiral Abel Aubert Dupetit-Thouars, commanding the Pacific naval base, supplied the answer in 1842. Cutting short the incredible saga of the "Pritchard Affair," he took the initiative of imposing a French protectorate on his friend Queen Pomaré, which made British blood boil and sent shivers down the spine of French diplomats.

THE MURDER OF A GOD

James Cook was killed on February 14, 1779, at Kealakeku Bay on the island of Owhyee (Hawaii). One theory holds that he was mistaken for Lono or Rono, the islanders' great white god of plenty who had returned, as had been prophesied, aboard the strange *pahi* that loomed into sight one morning. Cook was familiar with the Sandwich Islands, the Hawaiian archipelago. He had wintered here before continuing his exploration of the Bering Strait during his third voyage.

The ship set sail, but had to limp back with a broken foremast. Relations soon grew tense, building up until a pitched battle broke out. Cook, who was armed, had gone ashore to restore calm, but was mortally wounded. He was then torn to pieces in a kind of mystical frenzy, like a collective exorcism. "Our unfortunate commander was by the seaside when we saw him last; he was shouting at the boats and ordering them to cease fire and draw ashore so that our company could come

aboard. The naval forces and crew had opened fire before he had ordered it and he wanted to avoid additional bloodshed. As certain participants in the event testified, it seems that he fell victim to his own humanitarian concerns. It was observed indeed that, as long as he was facing the Hawaiians, they did not dare attack him, but as soon as he turned around to give orders, he was stabbed from behind and fell facedown into the sea. The Hawaiians shouted jubilantly when they saw he had fallen; they soon dragged his body ashore, and wielding daggers, they began to stab and club him with such ferocity, that they failed to notice that he was no longer breathing."

On February 18, toward eight o'clock in the evening, a pirogue was heard rowing toward the *Resolution*. The sentinels began shooting at it. The two men on the pirogue began shouting Tinee! (this is how they pronounced my name) and claiming that they were our friends. When they came aboard, they fell at our feet with extreme looks of fear. We recognized Tabu, the man who always accompanied Captain Cook. After shedding many tears, deploring the theft of the *Orono*, he gave us a package wrapped in material that he had tucked under his arm; I am incapable of expressing the sheer horror that gripped us when we saw that it was a piece of human flesh weighing approximately nine to ten pounds. This is what remained, they told us, of the body. They then asked us with a great tone of gravity what the *Orono* would do to them when it returned."

Cook's bones and hands were repatriated on the February 20. The following day, "Ihappu and the king's son came on board, bringing the remains of Captain Cook's bones, the barrel of his gun, his shoes, and a few small objects that belonged to him. Ihappu took great pains to convince us that Tirrïbu, Maïha-Maïha, and he wished from the bottom of their hearts for there to be peace." The story is excerpted from the diary of the lieutenant King. The bay was declared taboo, and the remains of the navigator were worshipped in Hawaii until pagan rites were abolished by Protestant pastors in the nineteenth century.

"We were going to kill them, as we thought they were evil spirits. But they offered a gift to our chief, which saved their lives." Ouallié, one of the chiefs of the village of Tanema in Vanikoro, recounted in 1827 the tale of Lapérouse's shipwreck

Left:
A shaman in Tahiti. Radiguet most likely was portraying a *tahua* (priest) or a charismatic chief with religious connotations, an *arii* or *arioi*.
Drawing with watercolor. Maximilien Radiguet album.

Right:
Mahiole. Crested helmet worn by chiefs of Hawaii, to identify them and as a means to signal their presence to the gods. A similar helmet was brought back from Cook's last voyage. Wicker and yellow and red feathers.
Brought back by Louis-François Le Goarant de Tromelin (1828).

Below:
Effigy of Ku-Kaili-Moku, war god of the Hawaiian Islands. Wicker statue decorated with mother of pearl and dog's teeth. It no longer has the original red feathers, the sacred color, which imbued it with divine powers. The effigy is said to have been brought back from Cook's expedition.

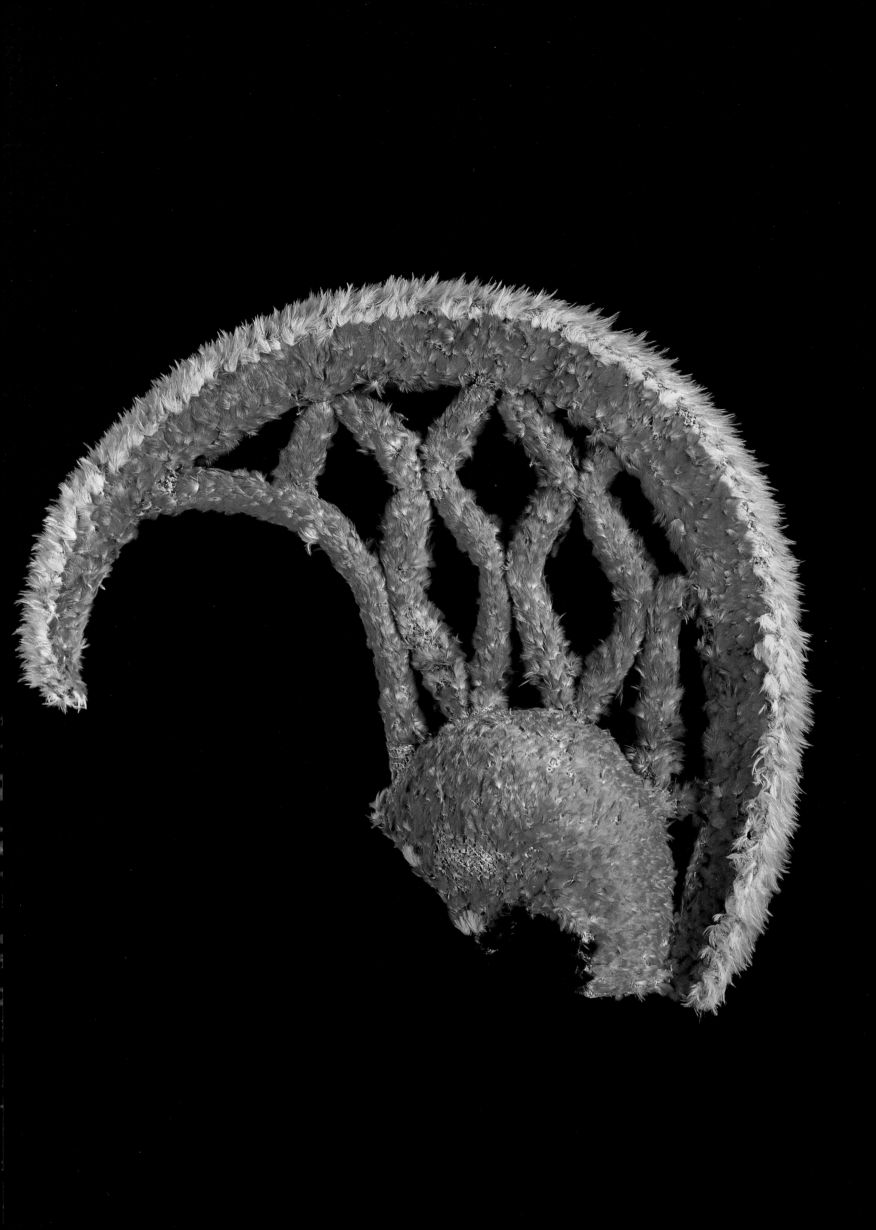

thirty-nine years earlier to a merchant captain. It loomed up on the horizon of the sea, from the immaculate regions where the tribal ancestors reside, triggering prophesies from the deepest oral traditions. The enormous pirogues that appeared out of nowhere radically altered knowledge deemed inviolate since time immemorial. To the islanders, the explorers were like extra-terrestrials. The natives were used to existing in harsh conditions, relying on instinct among the mangroves and coconut trees and living according to the rhythms of natural phenomena. The sight of the ships was jolting, and every sense went on full alert.

Village of Nama in Vanikoro. A guide for the village led Dumont d'Urville's officers in February 1828 to see the site of the shipwreck of Lapérouse's frigates, washed up forty years ago. Watercolor by Louis-Auguste de Sainjson, illustrator aboard the Dumont d'Urville's *Astrolabe* (1826-1829).

They saw beings come ashore who bore absolutely no resemblance to anything they had ever seen; nothing in their experience had prepared them for such a sight, except the oral narrators. On the beaches of the new land, two masked civilizations approached one another. Wallis interpreted the *ura-tatae* on the deck as being a peace offering; the bouquet of red feathers designated to appease the wrath of the gods. Given the tense atmosphere generated by the collision of these two worlds unknown to one another on the beaches, one friendly gesture, one knee-jerk insult, one sacrilegious faux-pas was all that was needed to determine if dialogue or a massacre would ensue. The seamen were undoubtedly on guard, given the tension among the crew, their cautious demeanor, and their acquaintance with the many myths, legends, and superstitions in dealing with initial contacts between populations with nothing in common. In addition, they most likely were troubled and distracted from maintaining close vigilance by the jarring opposition between the women's overt affections and demonstrations of friendship, and the signs of extreme savagery.

During Cook's second voyage, his companions witnessed scenes that were part of an unfathomable culture. The young naturalist Johann Georg Forster, who was an assistant to his father Johann Reinhold, wrote in June 1774 on the island of

A hostile reception by the natives of Opulu (Apia) in Samoa (1838) during Dumont d'Urville's second voyage. The aggressors of Lapérouse's expedition in Tutuila in 1787 came from Apia.
Lithograph from Louis Le Breton, illustrator and deputy surgeon aboard Dumont d'Urville's *Astrolabe* (second voyage from 1837-1840).

Nuka (Rotterdam) in the Tonga archipelago, where the *Resolution* had moored: "Each woman carried grapefruit and they gave us small pieces, displaying a great deal of tenderness and affection." He did not know that barely six months later, in Queen Charlotte's canal in New Zealand, ten crew members from the *Adventure* commanded by Tobias Furneaux, from whom they had no news, had been massacred and eaten while looking for edible plants, following a petty theft and an argument with the Maoris.

Second lieutenant James Burney described a horrible scene: "I looked about very carefully behind the beach to see if our canoe was there. I soon came upon a dreadful scene of carnage: the heads, hearts, and lungs of several of our people

Left:
Chief from Santa Christina
(Tahua Ta, Marquesa
archipelago). Engraving
after William Hodges,
painter and draftsman
of the *HMS Resolution*.

Right:
Marine officer and group
of Tahitian women. Voyage
of the *Reine Blanche*, of
Rear-Admiral Dupetit-
Thouars to the Marquesas
and to Tahiti. Drawing
with watercolor.
Maximilien Radiguet's
album.

Below:
Sculpted jamb-lining. New
Caledonia. These traditional
sculptures, typical of Kanak
art, were hung on either
side of the door of the
ancestors' huts.

were spread over the sand and, some distance off, dogs were digging through the entrails." These two dramatically diverse incidents were apparently quite routine, since Cook commented on them during his second voyage: "It was not rich in remarkable events."

Three years later, Cook passed by the site of the massacre and encountered Chief Kahoora, who had overseen it. Other Maoris explained in detail "without any trace of reserve" the conditions in which the tragic event took place, and "unanimously admired the fact that theft committed by their fellow men had sparked the argument; they agreed that the massacre had been a fortuitous event, and that if the crew had been less willing to punish the thief, no blood would have been shed." They maintained that, although they disliked Kahoora, they said, he could not be accused of having premeditated this ferocious carnage. According to Ferdinand de Lesseps, his uncle Barthelemy, a survivor of the Lapérouse expedition, told how Fleuriot de Langle, commander of the *Astrolabe*, a convoy of the *Boussole*, used to contemplate an engraving depicting Cook's tragic death hanging in his cabin and pensively remark: "This is the kind of death that anyone within our profession would wish." He was assassinated on December 11, 1787 in Tutuila in the Samoa archipelago.

Marc-Joseph Marion-Dufresne was killed in New Zealand, then eaten during a huge celebration, because a contingent of sailors had mistakenly cut down a sacred tree for kindling.

Left:
Watering up at the haven of Carteret (New Ireland). Watercolor by Louis-Auguste de Sainson. (Maiden voyage of Dumont d'Urville in 1826-1829.)

Below:
Papuan from Bougainville Island. René Primevère Lesson, a naturalist from Duperrey, searched zealously in 1823 and 1824 for birds of paradise in New Guinea, while his travel companions discovered the *Alfourous* and their impressive headdresses. Drawing with watercolor by L. F. Lejeune, illustrator aboard Louis-Isidore Duperrey's *Coquille* (1822-1825).

Right:
Native of Nuka Hiva (Nuku Hiva), Marquesa archipelago, 1838. Lithograph from Louis Le Breton, *Voyage to the South Pole and Oceanis.* Dumont d'Urville (1837-1840).

THE ENGLIGHTENMENT PUT TO THE TEST

Although they were not forewarned about the superficiality awaiting visitors in transit, the naval officers were curious observers, pragmatic and experienced. Their position and the experience of having traveled widely did not totally set them apart from their century, yet it freed them of certain prejudices and gave them a distanced perspective—particularly since they approached the various countries and inhabitants from aboard a ship, a spatial capsule isolated from the local context. The ship was an ideal laboratory of sorts for studying the social sciences. It would have been of great service if scientific inquiries into non-European cultures had been a salient concern at the time. Sailors often were opposed to armchair philosophers and geographers in the eighteenth century, as they had their own experiences with the so-called "noble savages" and "austral land"; the former often were right. Bougainville upbraided these philosophers harshly: "I am a traveler and sailor, in other words, a liar and imbecile in the eyes of the lazy and superb class of writers who, in the shadows of their dens, philosophize endlessly about the world and its inhabitants, imperiously subjugating nature to their imagination."

Cook and the naturalist Forster who accompanied him were highly appreciative of the Kanaks of New Caledonia, whom they discovered in 1774, and praised their ways of life endlessly. "We found them to be quite active, solid, civil, and peaceful; and we acknowledged one rare trait among the nations of this sea: they do not have even the slightest inclination to steal… The Caledonians are quite similar to the inhabitants of the Friendly Islands (Tonga Islands), but they are much gentler and amiable." The women were modest and free of any coquetry.

Unfortunately, the Englishmen's impressions were modified substantially some twenty years later in the haven of Balade, where Cook had moored, by Captain Elisabeth-Paul de Rossel, one of the survivors of the Entrecasteaux expedition that had set out to look for Lapérouse. "What is probably most surprising to those who

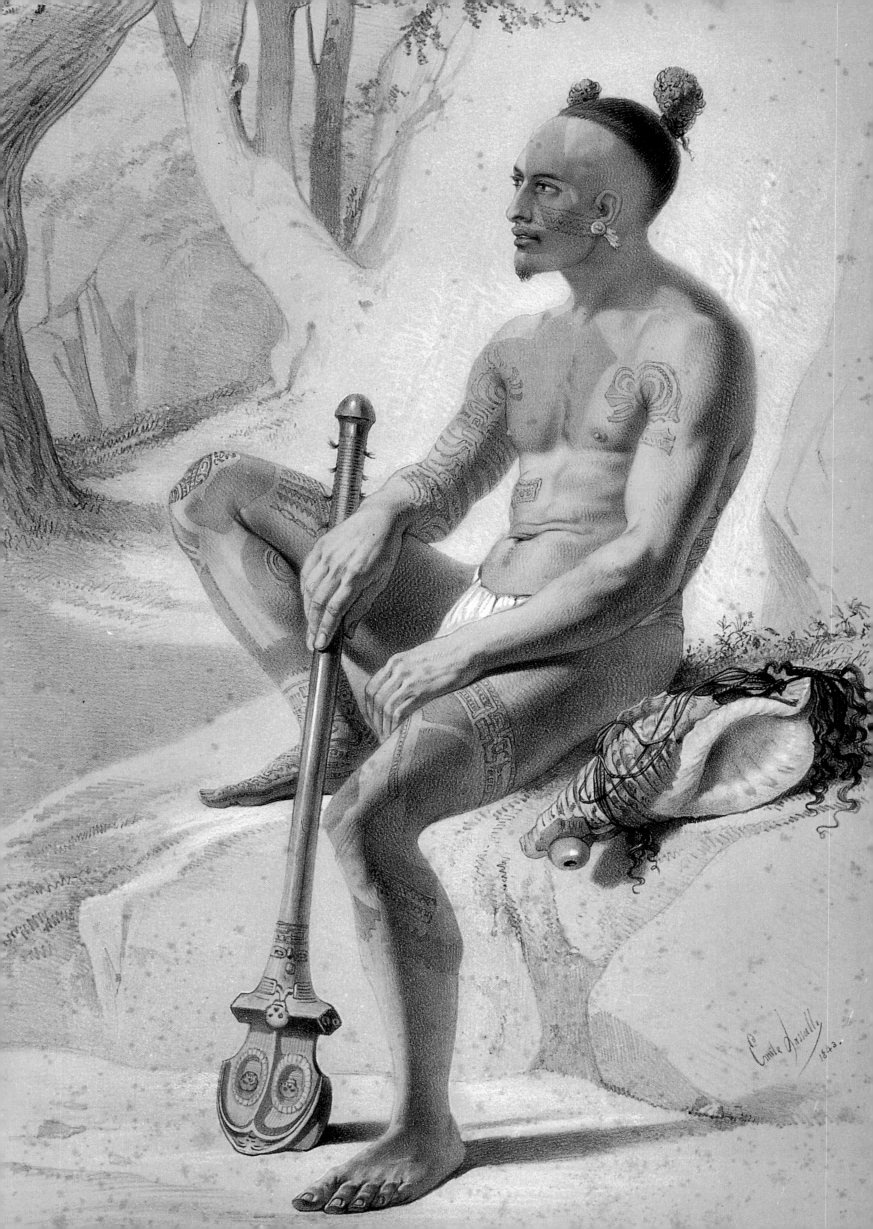

read the passages in which Mr. Forster paints such an enticing portrait of the simple ways of life and the humanity of the inhabitants of New Caledonia, is that the people are anthropophagus: they love human flesh, and are very open about it." The custom, as a ritual part of the culture, continued until the very recent past. Rossel described the circumstances in which the natives had identified on several occasions, with great disgust, pieces of grilled human flesh in the Kanaks' food.

There was therefore much evidence that if the natives seemed friendly at first, they were, in fact, fundamentally savage. Lapérouse was unequivocal about this after his stay on Easter Island in April 1786: "We approached them on their island only to bring good tidings; we gave them many presents; we showed great affection toward the weaker ones, particularly the suckling babes. We sowed a great variety of useful seeds in their fields; we left pigs, goats, and sheep in their dwellings that would quickly multiply; we asked for nothing in return. Nevertheless, they threw stones at us, and they stole just about everything that

wasn't nailed down." In late May, mooring off Mowee (Maui) in the Hawaiian Islands, where Cook was assassinated, and paying homage to the great navigator, Lapérouse tried again to be convinced of the civilizing impact of his mission: "Modern navigators, in describing the mores and customs of new civilizations, only seek to enrich the history of mankind. Their navigation must work toward completing the exploration of the entire globe, and the enlightenment they seek to spread have one goal: to make the islanders

I will at last admit, if it is so desired, that it is impossible for a society to exist without inherent virtues; but I am forced to acknowledge that I have not had the shrewdness to perceive them. They are always battling amongst themselves, neglecting their children, genuine tyrants with their wives, who are forced to toil endlessly at the most arduous tasks; I have seen nothing within this population that has softened the harsh tones of this image. (...) Philosophers would expostulate in vain. They write their books in sheltered corners by the hearth, and I have been traveling for thirty years. I have witnessed the injustices and wiles of these people, whom we have described as being so good, given their close relationship with nature; but nature is sublime only as a whole; the details are overlooked. It is impossible to enter the woods which the hand of civilized man has not pruned; to cross plains that are littered with rocks and stones, and flooded with unpractical swamps; to associate with native men, for they are barbaric, nasty, and knavish.

Jean-François de Galaup de Lapérouse.

July 1786, after his expedition to Alaska.

Posthumous edition of *Voyage de Lapérouse autour du monde*, 1797.

they have visited happier, as they have increased their means of subsistence, planted trees, sown grain in every country, and brought iron tools."

He repeated his feeling of powerlessness two months later, after observing the people of Tlingit in Alaska.

On January 1, 1787, arriving in Macao, Robert de Lamanon, a naturalist and physicist working with Lapérouse, wrote to Maréchal de Castries, Minister of the Navy: "In the early years of the past century, our neighbors discovered a New World to find gold; this century, the French charted the shape and dimensions of the Earth using measurements…; but what sets this voyage apart from the others, and will always be a source of glory for the French nation in the eyes of philosophers today and to come, will be having frequented civilizations considered barbaric without one drop of blood being spilled." He added as a prescient post-script, "The campaign for truth is not over." On December 11 of that same year, Lamanon, Fleuriot de Langle commanding the *Astro-labe*, and a dozen men were assassinated in Maouna (Tuitila) in the Samoa Islands as they were watering up, by a band of natives from a neighboring island who had come to test these so-called "invulnerable" foreigners.

In the heat of the emotion stirred up by the calamity that had struck his expedition, Lapérouse wrote: "My opinion of the uncivilized peoples was determined long ago; my voyage only confirmed what I thought. (…) I learned all too well about them, at my peril. I am however a thousand times angrier at the philosophers who idealize the savages, than I am at the savages themselves. Poor Lamanon, whom they massacred, said to me the very night before his death, that these men were far superior to us. I have always strictly observed the orders I have been given, yet I have carried them out with a great deal of moderation. I do swear, however, that if I were to undertake a new campaign similar to this one, I would request other orders. A navigator leaving Europe must consider the savages as enemies, very weak in truth, and it would be far from generous to launch an attack without any motive, and would be barbaric to destroy, but that we must have the right to pre-empt any such incidents, when we have even the slightest suspicions of them. I still have many interesting things to accomplish, hostile

Left:
*Inaugurating the Cenotaph
Erected in Vanikoro by the
Crew of Dumont d'Urville's*
Astrolabe, *in Homage to
the Lapérouse Expedition.*
March 1828.
Watercolor by
Louis-Auguste de Sainson.
(Dumont d'Urville's first
voyage in 1826-1829.)

civilizations to visit: I am not saying that we should shoot cannons at them; for I am thoroughly convinced that fear alone can halt the impact of their evil intentions."

After a final stopover in Botany Bay near what is today Sydney, the Lapérouse expedition broke up in March 1788. Wreckage was found forty years later in Vanikoro, in the Salomon archipelago in Melanesia, where oral tradition maintained that two ships hit the shore during the night of a terrible tropical storm. It seems likely that the survivors, who were exhausted by the deleterious climate of the island and brought with them a variety of esoteric and precious objects, tools and weapons, were massacred as they left the lagoon in search of land frequented by Europeans aboard a makeship boat they had built. No substantial proof has ever been found, in Vanikoro or elsewhere, of the second death of the Lapérouse expedition. And then, the chaos subsided, and the paroxysms that had plunged some of the scientific voyages into a world of horror during the last quarter of the eighteenth century were relegated to oblivion. The contact between Europe and its philosophers and the natives of blissful islands had been established.

Kava ceremony in Tonga-Tabu (April 1827). One of the Tonga-Tabu chiefs offered Dumont d'Urville's crew some kava, a ceremonial plant-derived beverage that is fermented. Lithograph by Nicolas Noël from a watercolor by Louis-Auguste de Sainson. (Dumont d'Urville's first voyage in 1826-1829.)

Background image: Native and mother-of-pearl masks from the island of Aroub, Strait of Torres. Atlas of Dumont d'Urville's voyage.

The ignorance of the origins of the Maoris was one of the biggest misunderstandings of the Pacific exploration. Western observers logically saw the peoples of the Pacific as aborigines. Cook harbored suspicions as to their navigation skills. "The great [pirogues] seem very difficult to handle, yet they are skilled experts at doing so. I believe that they undertake long voyages to faraway places aboard these boats, or they would not have any knowledge as to the islands located in these seas." The intellectual prejudices of the Europeans masked a remarkable fact: New Zealanders, Tahitians, Easter Islanders, Kanaks, and Tongans had been long-distance navigators since time immemorial. The various waves of Maori settlers, who had come from the Philippines twenty-five centuries before the birth of Christ, had crossed Melanesia and spread out over the Tonga Islands in Hawaii, between 500 BC and the year 1,000, and to New Zealand in the mid-eleventh century. They landed in South America before the Spanish did. The Maoris were colonizers of the world's largest oceans, and had some twenty centuries' advancement over Europe's special envoys sent during the Enlightenment.

Greek geographers in the fourth century B.C. had already determined that the Earth was round; one century later, they discovered that it revolved around the sun. Alexander the Great's surveyors and the early navigators adventured furtively beyond the Pillars of Hercules, what we now call the Strait of Gibraltar, and began to sketch the outlines of the world around the Mediterranean Sea. The eighteenth- and nineteenth-century scholarly explorers completed a quest that had begun during Homer's time. Armed with a few bronze and crystal instruments, immersed in their books riddled with tropical insects, these field scientists persisted stubbornly in their efforts to collect information, although many were feverish and weakened by the deplorable sanitary conditions. Now that the world is encircled by a myriad of satellites and almost every corner of the planet can been reached by tourists of some sort, we seem to have all forgotten that just one hundred and fifty years ago, the Earth was still poorly explored and distances uncertain. Sometimes forgotten, too, is that this information was gathered with much difficulty and through the exhausting efforts—even to the point of self-sacrifice—of scholars and navigators wholeheartedly to the methodic investigation of the world and its natural laws.

Frigates were given instructions to fly their colors with dignity, particularly in the South Seas. Eighteenth-century exploratory expeditions by sea were designed as scientific missions, carrying aboard ship astronomers, who were to set up their instruments as portable observatories. The leaders and chief officers of these expeditions were extremely well-versed in nautical astronomy. This knowledge helped in understanding the physical and human geography of the southern hemisphere and in the exploration of the unknown regions that remained in the

Preceding double page:
Transplanting Tahiti
breadfruit trees.
This was the beginning
of the famous *Bounty* story.
William Bligh was
commissioned to transport
breadfruit trees from
Tahiti to the West Indies.
The mutiny broke out
on April 28, 1789.
Lithograph by
Thomas Gosse, 1796.

Left:
Humboldt in his
Orianenburgstrasse
library in Berlin.
Lithography by Ernst
Hildbrant, 1856.

Right:
Collection of tropical shells.
The immense collection
of exotic objects and
specimens brought back
to Europe from scientific
expeditions launched
a fashion for curio
collections in the second
half of the sixteenth century.
Gouache by Alexandre-
Isidore Leroy de Barde,
1803. This artist painted
six works illustrating natural
history collections for
Louis XVIII.

Below.
Sea lion.
Australian school,
circa 1840.

Australian lyre bird.
Gouache by John William
Lewin (1780-1819).

We saw in the woods a tree bearing
a fruit the color and shape of
a cherry; its juice was sour and
pleasant, though somewhat tasteless.
The woods were separated by the
most beautiful meadows in the world…
In the evening, the skiff returned
from fishing with two sting rays,
which together weighed nearly
six hundred pounds. Mr. Banks and
Doctor Solander found such a large
number of plants here that I named
it Botany Bay. It is situated at 34° 0' S
and 208°37' W. It is spacious, safe,
and practical. It can be recognized by
the land, which is relatively low
and uniform around the coast.

James Cook, May 5, 1770.
Log from the first voyage (1768-1771).

immense emptiness of the Pacific Ocean. James Cook, who made three extraordinary voyages, can be credited for most of these discoveries. Lapérouse's tragic expedition had been expected to fill in the remaining gaps. It was neither planned nor undertaken with the same brilliance or efficiency as Cook's, but it would have been useful from a scientific point of view—had it not suffered from such a disastrous fate. Despite wars and crises, the special envoys sent from Europe throughout the world were all accorded diplomatic status, in the name of science. Louis XVI had given his ships orders to consider Cook as a benefactor of humanity. The Prussian statesman Humboldt traveled with a French passport, which declared that he was "traveling in the name of knowledge."

OCEAN-GOING NATURALISTS

Philibert Commerson was the first naturalist asked to participate in a worldwide expedition, to give it a more scientific dimension. He paid tribute to Bougainville by naming a plant after him: "an admirable plant, with sumptuous, large flowers that adorned many houses" in Rio and Montevideo.

In 1768, Cook embarked a team of naturalists and illustrators under the supervision of Joseph Banks. They were overwhelmed by the discoveries made during their voyage, during which they detected and catalogued plants and food crops in Tahiti, "all these products which the earth offers them almost spontaneously," as well as sweet potatoes, yams, mangoes, sugar cane, and other local species, which the Polynesians called *pia, ti, ihi, fara, teve,* and *nono.*

Because of the immense number of previously unknown species, a bay in New Holland (present-day Australia) received a special name: Botany Bay. This bay in New South Wales, which Cook claimed for England, is today the site of the small town of Lapérouse, a suburb of Sydney. Lapérouse made his last known port of call in Botany Bay in 1788, at the same time Commodore Philips was settling Port Jackson, the first inhabited colony in Australia, in a nearby, although deeper bay.

It was during repairs to the *Endeavour,* which had scraped a coral reef, that the crew saw "an animal as large as a hare, extremely agile, and with a thin body." Cook himself caught a glimpse of this creature several days later. "By its

Johann Reinhold Forster and his son Johann Georg. These Prussians of Scottish origin were naturalists and natural history illustrators on Cook's second voyage (1772-1775).

Spanner crab, which lives in the West Pacific and in the Indian Ocean. Watercolor by William Ellis, assistant surgeon and natural history illustrator on Cook's third voyage (1776-1780).

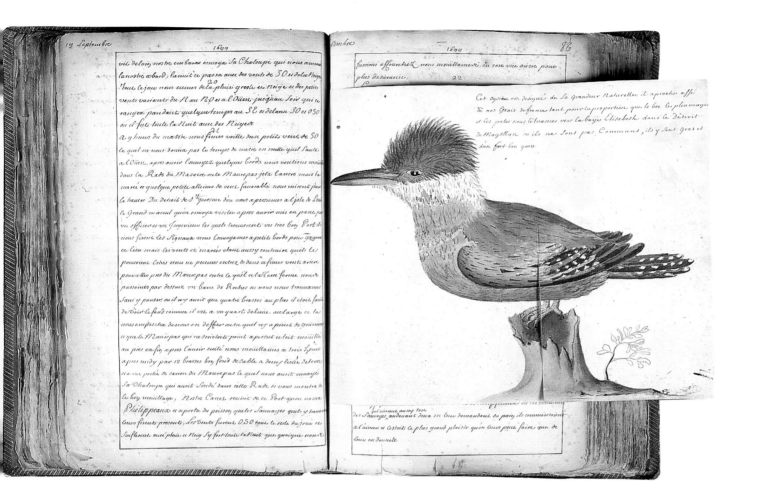

Bird from the Strait of
Magellan. September 1699.
Manuscript journal by
Duplessis, Beauchesne's
cartographer and engineer
aboard the *Maurepas*
(1698-1701).

size and appearance, it resembled a hare. It also had a long tail, and I would have taken it for a wild dog, if, instead of running, it had not jumped like a hare or a deer. Mr. Banks did not get a clear look at this animal, and he thought that its species was as yet unknown." Sidney Parkinson, a botanical illustrator (who would later die during the voyage, as would his colleague Alexander Buchan, a landscape painter), sketched the first image of a kangaroo.

The collection of botanical rarities continued apace during the second voyage, with a stop at New Caledonia, where on Île des Pins, they found the astonishing monkey-puzzle trees, which look like bearded telephone poles and were named *Araucaria columnaris* or the araucaria of Norfolk Island. Other discoveries included the *Howea forsteriana*, the Antarctic beech, the *Barringtonia speciosa* of Tahiti, and thousands of other unknown plants and shrubs. Although ethnologists would become specialists in this field in the distant future, others scientists, including zoologists, entomologists, and botanists, were happily buried under the avalanche of hundreds of thousands of specimens—including thousands that had never before been identified. Jean-Jacques de La Billardière, a naturalist with d'Entrecasteaux, planted a *Eucalyptus globulus* found in Tasmania in a garden in Malmaison, a suburb of Paris. Just fifty years later, the eucalyptus would become

Dessin d'un Poisson volant qui tomba la nuit dans le Vaisseau de sa grandeur Naturelle

Ton donnant Chasse aux Poissons volants

Tuna hunting flying fish.

Aholeholes.
Cape Verde Islands.
Manuscript journal by Duplessis, cartographer and engineer on Jacques Gouin de Beauchesne's voyage to Peru via the Strait of Magellan in 1698-1701, for the South Seas Trading Company.

Tiger cat from New South Wales. Lithograph by Jean-Dominique-Étienne Canu (1807), from a watercolor by Charles Alexandre Lesueur (1802). *Voyage de découvertes aux terres australes* (Scientific Expedition to the Southern Lands) by Commander Nicolas Baudin. Lesueur was one of the painters and illustrators aboard the *Naturaliste* and the *Géographe,* which sailed around Australia in 1800-1804.

Top right:
Kangaroos (*Macropus giganteus*).
Gouache by Charles-Alexandre Lesueur (1802).

Bottom right:
Bat.
Watercolor by William Ellis.
James Cook's third voyage (1776-1780).

Paca.

a common plant in the Mediterranean basin, from France to North Africa.

Nicolas Baudin's expedition in the early years of the nineteenth century to the Australian coast was inauspicious from the start. Desertions, violent tensions, a health debacle, and repeated insubordination exposed the unpopularity of a leader who was brutal and curiously stubborn, despite his experience. When he returned via Île de France (Mauritius) in August 1803, Baudin had transformed the *Géographe* into a zoo and botanical garden. The observations and drawings (including 1,500 drawn from life by Charles Alexandre Lesueur), along with the herbs, insects, plants, and living animals they gathered covered more than 100,000 specimens, including 25,000 that were previously unknown. Cuvier was impressed with these collections as well as with the additional studies into the behavior and habits of these species.

Ethnographers and anthropologists were delighted with the observations and drawings, which provided valuable eye-witness accounts of the aborigines. During their voyage, the *Géographe* and the *Naturaliste* had encountered *Investigator,* captained by Matthew Flinders, who came up with the name for Australia. The two French frigates stayed at sea for periods exceeding one hundred days at least four different times, a length of time beyond which scurvy became fatal. The ship put into the Dutch island of Timor from August to November 1801—where, perniciously, scurvy was replaced by dysentery. When Baudin was finally enlightened as to his errors in terms of his crew's health (thanks to advice from English sailors), it was too late for his exhausted and prematurely aged men. He would also pass away on September 16, 1803 on Île de France, surrounded by his ill and dying crew.

Some thirty years later, Auguste Nicolas Vaillant undertook a two-year voyage aboard the *Bonite;* a dozen other such missions sailed at the same time. The scientific results of his trip would not be published for another twenty-six years. Waterloo and Napoleon's exile to Saint Helena put an end to the Empire's great adventure. The war that had swept through all of

Left:
Mororé aborigine in New Holland (Australia).

Below:
Woman from Bruny Island south of Van Diemen's Land (Tasmania). New Holland was the Dutch name for Australia, where the British occupied only the eastern coast (New South Wales). Watercolors by Nicolas-Martin Petit, Baudin's painter and illustrator.

Right:
Title page from the historical and navigational log of the ship's captain, Nicolas Baudin, commander in chief of the corvettes *Géographe* and *Naturaliste* (1800-1801).

Journal du *Capitaine* de *Vaisseau* N.re

Baudin Commandant en Chef les *Corvettes* le

Géographe et le *Naturaliste*, Destinées par le *Gouvernement* à faire

une Campagne de *Reconnoissances* et de *Recherches* dans Différentes Parties

des *Mers Australes*.

Chapitre Premier.

Motifs qui ont donné lieu à faire cette Campagne. Raisons pour lesquelles le Directoire Exécutif
après en avoir adopté le Plan en a Ajourné l'Exécution. Moyens employés pour Décider le Nouveau Gouvernement
à s'en Occuper. Mémoire Présenté et Lu à l'Institut National dans les Séances des Seize et Dix sept Pluviose

Europe for twenty years was over. Just after the Treaty of Paris was signed, the French Minister of the Navy presented a program for distant explorations to the government. From 1817 to 1839, no fewer than nine expeditions set sail for the South Pacific.

France, like England for twenty years, maintained an almost permanent maritime presence in the area in the form of at least one—and sometimes two or even three—frigates through 1838, sent to research the area. These missions were captained by such men as Louis-Claude de Saulses de Freycinet aboard his *Uranie;* Louis Isidore Duperrey on *Coquille;* Pierre-Théodore Laplace, then Ferdinand Hamelin, on the *Favorite;* Auguste Nicolas Vaillant and the *Bonite;* Abel Aubert Dupetit-Thaours aboard the *Vénus;* Jules Dumont d'Urville on the *Astrolabe;* Jean-Baptiste Cécille aboard the *Héroine;* and Laplace on the *Artémise.* In 1839, the *Erebus* and *Terror* set sail for Antarctica under the command of James Clark Ross.

Russian expeditions, pursuing the ambitious maritime projects of Peter the Great in the eighteenth century, particularly the voyages toward Kamchatka and the Kuril Islands, continued to explore the North Pacific and the regions around the Antarctic from 1803 to 1829 under the orders of Adam Ivan von Krusenstern, Otto von Kotzebue, Fabian Bellingshausen, and Fedor Petrovich Lutke.

In the nineteenth century, the discovery of indigenous people was no longer a priority. The orders given to one of de Freycinet's frigate captains in 1817 no longer included instructions to study "the customs of untamed peoples." Instead, they stressed the collection of scientific information, which would offer a new way of looking at natural history and life, at a time when scientists were moving past a mere cataloguing of species to a reflection on the organization of the

Charles Darwin. Portrait by George Richmond, 1840. Darwin was returning from his trip aboard the *Beagle,* commanded by Robert Fitz-Roy (1831-1836).

Below:
Lobipes lobatus or northern phalarope. Watercolor by William Ellis. James Cook's third voyage (1776-1780).

natural realm. In 1809, Jean-Baptiste de Lamarck introduced the idea of transformism. Georges Cuvier and Geoffroy Saint-Hilaire had been debating their ideas for some time already. In 1836, Charles Darwin, a humble Cambridge student, embarked at the last minute to replace his teacher aboard Robert Fitz-Roy's *Beagle*, back from a long voyage. Just twenty-seven years old, he was about to overturn the firmly entrenched scientific and Christian beliefs concerning the origins of species.

Sizing up the world

Determining longitude was a problem that first interested the ancient Greeks. Much later, in the 1760s and 1770s, after large observatories had been constructed and the Longitude Act had been signed into law in Great Britain, two separate disciplines worked toward developing techniques for measuring longitude at sea: astronomy and clockmaking. The difficulty in measuring longitude is due to the rotation of the Earth around its axis. The difference in longitude between two points on the globe form an hour angle, determined by the simple relationship between the local time zones, as the sun sweeps over the 360° of the Earth's longitude in a twenty-four hour period.

Only two methods exist to determine, using natural or mechanical means, the difference in time zones. The first consists of carrying a timepiece set to the original meridian or point or departure, which can then be compared with the sun's

Map of the Indian Ocean by Bertrand-François Mahé de La Bourdonnais, 1750. An officer in the East India Trading Company, appointed governor of the Île de France (Mauritius) and Bourbon (Reunion) in 1734, he left an enduring legacy in the Indian Ocean. Drawing sketched on a handkerchief.

Background: Configuration of an island seen on March 17, 1792. D'Entrecasteaux's ships, *Recherche* and *Espérance*, were then sailing in the region of the Saint Paul and Amsterdam islands, heading toward Tasmania under heavy seas. Drawing by Dom Pierson, astronomer serving as chaplain aboard the *Espérance*.

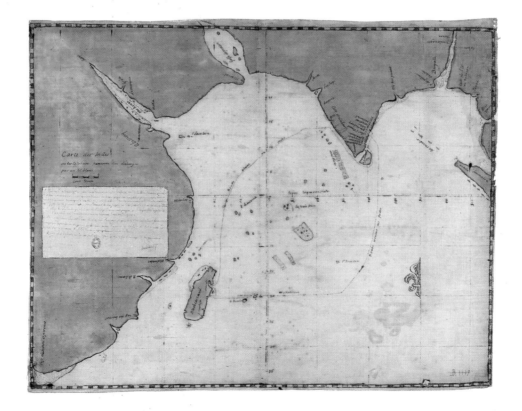

INTRODUCTION
HISTORIQUE:
ou
JOURNAL DES TRAVAUX
DES ACADEMICIENS
Envoyés par ordre du Roi sous l'Équateur:
Depuis 1735 jusqu'en 1745.

Tous ceux qui ont pris quelque part à la question de la Figure de la Terre, ont remarqué avec surprise que dix ans ont à peine suffi pour terminer notre voyage. On en avoit estimé la durée à quatre tout au plus : encore supposoit-on alors, conformément au premier projet, qu'outre la mesure

PREMIÈRE PARTIE.
MESURE GÉOMÉTRIQUE
DE L'ARC DU MERIDIEN,
ou
OPERATIONS SUR LE TERREIN,
Pour fixer la position & déterminer la longueur de
la Ligne Méridienne.

J'ai cru que le meilleur moyen de présenter au Lecteur avec clarté & précision le détail d'un grand nombre de différentes opérations, étoit de former une Table qui rassemblant sous un point de vûe le plus d'objets qu'il seroit possible.

position at the zenith, which indicates noon in the second place. The problem was to construct a timepiece that, if it could not keep exact time, could at least remain regular during the weeks and months at sea, despite a ship's movement and the effects of climatic changes (humidity, heat, and so on). In the mid-eighteenth-century, no timepiece yet existed that could meet the needs of the navigators.

The second method consists in observing the local time using specific astronomical phenomena, and then consulting an ephemeris to calculate the time at which the same configuration was or would be visible at the original meridian or point of departure. The only natural phenomena visible throughout the entire world are astronomical. In practice, there were two variations of this method, each of which had its own particular problem: on the one hand, the scarcity of eclipses and the need to use telescopes that were too large to be carried on board ships; and on the other, the need for tables and extremely precise measuring instruments.

Astronomers and clockmakers achieved operational results almost simultaneously. Navigators, working to rectify and define the maps of the world, were impressed at the spectacular progress. During Cook's second voyage around the world, he had an exact copy of the first operational chronometer ever made, a timepiece that took John Harrison thirty years to develop. Cook paid tribute to the clock, calling it his "trusted guide," and thanked the inventors once he had returned to port: "I would not be doing justice to Mr. Harrison or Mr. Kendall if I did not acknowledge the very great help I received from this timepiece."

Lapérouse, who took chronometers made by Ferdinand Berthoud aboard his ship, was also delighted with the results: "We are justified in concluding that the mean results for determining longitude by observing the distances of the sun and moon could not have been erroneous by more than one quarter of a degree. We no

Title page of a report by Charles-Marie de La Condamine concerning the measurement of a meridian arc (1751). The triangulation operations directed by the astronomer Louis Godin took place from 1736 to 1743 in Ecuador. A similar mission was underway in Lapland; the goal was to check the flatness of the Earth.

Below:
Survey and view of the coast of Timor Island on October 21, 1792. D'Entrecasteaux was looking for evidence of the Lapérouse expedition between New Guinea and the island of Celebes, as he sailed through an insalubrious environment that would decimate his crew.
Drawing by Dom Pierson, astronomer serving as chaplain aboard the *Espérance*.

Pages from the *Espérance* ship's log, October 19 and 20, 1792, maintained by Dom Pierson.

Vue prise a 6.ᵖ 20.ᵐ du matin le 21 8ᵇʳᵉ 1792

Configuration d'une partie de la Côte N.O. de l'Isle de Timor suivie depuis 6.ʰ 20.ᵐ du Matin jusqu'à 6.ᵖ

Vue d'une partie N.O de l'Isle de Timor prise à 9ʰ Du Matin le 21 8ᵇʳᵉ 1792

longer had to fear the limited error or uncertainty that could result from imperfections in the lunar tables. We were thus able to use the results of these operations confidently and repeatedly almost every day, observing the regularity of the marine chronometer by comparing it to the first results. All the many repeated precautions we took assure me that our determinations achieved a degree of accuracy that deserves the confidence of scholars and navigators." Lapérouse added an enthusiastic conclusion to his report: "We must note here the astonishing accuracy of these new methods; in less than one century, every point on Earth shall have been assigned its exact position, and have advanced geography more than in all centuries gone by."

Lapérouse's last known letter, given to the British who were settling Sydney, was addressed to Charles-Pierre Claret de Fleurieu, who planned the voyage and was one of the pioneers of scientific navigation. He returned to the subject of the new parameters in navigation. "I need merely tell you that the combination of our two methods, marine chronometers and the observations of distances, has completely solved the problem: we constantly sailed with less error in longitude that we had in latitude ten years ago."

With the puzzle of longitude solved and improved cartographic methods, one of the routine tasks on these scientific expeditions was to add any information that would be useful to navigation, with a priority for the physical makeup of the globe and the Earth's magnetic field, which were fundamental to the use of the compass and to compensate for compass errors. Flinders had returned to England with the experimental bases for understanding magnetic deviation and errors in steering compasses. Navigation had become an almost exact science.

Dessiné d'après nature
Par Duché de Vancy
en Juillet
1786.

Travelers during this period rectified maps, removing mythical islands and assigning to each landmass its proper position on the map of the world. They themselves were navigating with faulty maps, and were the last to run such risks. In 1788, several weeks after leaving the coast of Australia, Laperouse's *Astrolabe* and *Boussole* smashed on the rocks of one of the last unknown islands in the Pacific: Vanikoro.

STORMS

Accidents at sea were common during the days of sailing ships, particularly in areas of the Pacific Ocean that were studded with coral reefs. Ship logs are filled with alarming accounts. Lapérouse experienced the first of these crises in July of 1786. His ship had been driven off course by a violent current just as he was entering the Port-des-Français (Lituya Bay) fjord in Alaska to anchor. "In the thirty years I have spent at sea, I have never before seen two ships come so close to being lost." He ordered sailors to sound the pass before returning to sea. "At ten in the morning, I saw our small skiff return. Somewhat surprised, as I did not expect it to return so quickly, I asked M. Boutin, before he was lifted aboard, if something had happened. At the time, I feared an attack of some sort by savages: M. Boutin did not look reassuring; the greatest pain was reflected on his face."

Lieutenant Charles-Marie de Boutin, who was commanding the three skiffs sent out to sound the pass, reported back to his captain of being brutally carried away by the breaking waves. "In an instant, I was in the middle of the largest waves, which were almost filling up the boat. Yet it didn't sink and I could

Top left:
Interior of Port-des-Français. Ink wash drawing by Blondela, illustrator aboard the *Astrolabe.*

Bottom left:
View of the end of Port-des-Français, northwest America. Ink wash drawing by Duché de Vancy, landscapist aboard the *Boussole.* Lapérouse's voyage (1785-1788). The two frigates stayed at Port-des-Français (Lituya Bay) in Alaska from July 3 to 30, 1786. Lapérouse was looking for the Northwest Passage, a persistent goal throughout the eighteenth century.

Right:
Louis XVI Giving Instructions to Lapérouse on June 26, 1785. Behind the king stands the Maréchal de Castries, secretary of the navy, holding a copy of the *King's Statement to be Used as Specific Instructions to Monsieur de La Pérouse.* Louis XVI took a close personal interest in the organization of the voyage. Painting by Nicolas-André Monsiau (1817).

Preceding double page:
*Shipwreck of Launches
at Port-des-Français.*
On July 13, 1786, three
small craft sent to survey
the Port-des-Français pass
were swept toward an
extremely violent bar,
resulting in the death
of twenty-one officers,
sailors, and soldiers.
Painting by Louis-Philippe
Crépin (1772-1851).

Left:
*Impressive Icebergs,
Near inaccessible islands.*
In January 1838, the
Astrolabe and the *Zélée*,
encountered the impassable
ice floes that covered
Weddell Sea in the South
Atlantic Ocean when
they reached latitude 65° S.
Lithograph from Louis
Le Breton. Atlas of Dumont
d'Urville's second voyage
(1837-1840).

Right:
View and map of Matthew
Island in the Coral Sea,
by ship mate Pierre-Édouard
Guilbert aboard the
Astrolabe. January 1828.
Atlas of Dumont d'Urville's
first voyage (1826-1829).

continue to steer so that I could also face the waves, which gave me the greatest hope of escaping this danger. Our biscayner moved away from me while I dropped the grappling anchor, and several minutes later was in the breakers. The last I saw, the first waves were breaking over it, but during a moment when I was at the top of these breakers, I saw it again underwater, at thirty or forty fathoms in front; it was sideways. I could not see any men or oars... M. de Marchainville was a quarter league inside the pass when I was carried away; I have not seen him since that moment, but all those who know him know what his noble and generous character inspired him to do. It is probable that, when he saw our two boats in the middle of the breakers, not understanding how we were carried along, he assumed that either we had lost our oars or a small cable had snapped. In an instant, he would have rowed to reach us at the start of the first breakers. Seeing us struggle in the midst of the waves, he would have listened only to his own courage, and he would have tried to cross the breakers to come to our aid from outside, at the risk of perishing with us." Fifteen crewmen and six young officers, including the two La Borde brothers, drowned. The voyage had only just begun.

D'Entrecasteaux, sent on orders from the French Assemblée Constituante eight years later to search for Lapérouse, almost foundered on the reefs that stretch to the south of New Caledonia. "At daybreak, we found ourselves surrounded by reefs: the space we had in order to tack our way out was very short; the wind was strong and the seas heavy. We tried to come about into the wind three times to avoid danger, and which was not more than five cable lengths away. Three times, the heavy swells turned us off course, before we could come up into the wind. We made a fourth attempt, easing off the foresail sheet so that we could come about more quickly. This method worked and it was nigh time, as we would not have had the room necessary to run with a tailwind, even by backing the head sails."

Le Volcan Mathew à trois milles et demi de distance et au Nord du Monde.

Dumont d'Urville was also searching for Lapérouse and indeed was about to find his shipwrecked boat when he, too, almost smashed his *Astrolabe* on the reefs of Tonga-Tabou, after a violent wind drove his ship onto the reef. Their situation was catastrophic for two days, until an unexpected shift in the tide refloated the frigate. Concern quickly gave way to a revived enthusiasm for the mission. "Just two days ago, I would have been as happy as I could be to simply escape from the reefs and sail immediately to some port in Chile or Peru to repair our damage. Now that I have been helped by good fortune, I desire nothing so much as to continue the voyage, as if I had not experienced any setback at all."

The Maori seemed to take endless pleasure from the sea; they were constantly on the water, aboard their outrigger canoes, which whirled like mosquitoes around the European frigates at anchor. This ease was especially disconcerting considering that bathing in the sea was still a daunting adventure. Jules Michelet advised against this practice in 1861 unless proper precautions were taken, and it was only undertaken under the watchful eye of skilled swimmers.

In 1774, Cook saw something that looked to be an impressive war fleet in Tahiti. His painter, William Hodges, created a famous painting of the great battle *pahi*. "The warships consisted of 160 large double pirogues, fully equipped with men and weapons. The leaders, in other words, all those on the combat platforms, were in battle dress: this meant many thick cloth turbans, breastplates and helmets, some of which were so large that they prevented the person wearing it from moving about freely. It mattered little, as it added indubitably to the grandeur of this demonstration in which they flaunted their advantage with a certain satisfaction, on their boats decorated with flags and banners. All this created the grandest and proudest appearance that we had ever seen on these seas. The pirogues were lined up tightly one against another, the afts toward the coastline and the sterns pointing toward the sea; the chief's boat was, as well as I could gauge, in the center. In addition to these pirogues, there were one hundred seventy other boats, smaller

Tahitian war boats.
The large O-Too fleet,
assembled at O-Parae
(Tahiti).
Painting by William Hodges,
1774.

Background:
Portrait of Nataï,
New Zealand chief, 1827.
Lithograph by Sainson
and Maurin, 1833.
Atlas of Dumont d'Urville's
first voyage (1826-1829).

Fijian pirogue under shelter
on Vava'u Island, 1827.
Lithograph from
Louis-August de Saison.
Atlas of Dumont d'Urville's
first voyage (1826-1829).

double pirogues, all with a cover and rigged with masts and sails, most likely intended for transport, supplies, and to received wounded fighters."

The Maori had other nautical entertainment besides water tournaments and war. James King, second lieutenant aboard the *Resolution*, who finished Cook's log after the great explorer was assassinated on Owhyhee (Hawaii) in 1779, wrote an incredulous description of their nautical games on Karakuoa Bay: "When, in stormy weather, the raging surf has reached its peak, they take advantage of the moment to enjoy the pleasures of this game. Twenty or thirty men each take a long narrow piece of wood, which has been rounded off at each end; they leave the beach together and dive under the first wave they encounter. When, after much effort, they have managed to swim beyond the surf where the sea is calmer, they then get on their boards and prepare to return to the shore. The surf consists of several waves; the third one is always larger than the first two and goes farther… Their goal is to catch the top of this wave, which propels them to the beach with astonishing speed." Lieutenant King was explaining the ease with which the Hawaiians surfed, due in large part to the fact that even young children could already swim like fish.

A HELLISH JOURNEY

From late September 1787 to late January 1788, Lapérouse crossed the Pacific for the third time, from Kamchatka to the landmass that would be called Australia. The four-month crossing was interrupted only by a few days spent on the Solomon Islands. The small ships, worn out by more than two years at sea, were constantly rolled from side to side by the giant swells that damaged the masts and made the crew sick. Fatigue set in, as evidenced by the lines in the expedition leader's log. "September 27. Can anyone believe that hardtack eaten by worms as sometimes happens and resembling a beehive, meat corroded by acrid salt, and utterly

desiccated and spoiled vegetables can provide sustenance in our weakened state?"

"November 6. We are extremely tired by rough eastern rollers which, like those in the Atlantic Ocean, reign constantly over this vast sea, and we have found neither bonito nor dorado; at best, we have caught a glimpse of a few flying fish.

"November 9. The heat is oppressive, and the hygrometer has never before recorded such a high level of humidity since we left Europe. We are breathing heavy air which, combined with poor food, has weakened our energy and made us practically unable to perform any hard work if circumstances should so require it.

"November 21. Nothing breaks the monotony of this long crossing. A vast solitude reigns all around us; the air and water in this part of the globe have no inhabitants.

"November 23. Heavy swells from the west make sailing extremely wearying: our ropes, rotted from the constant humidity that we have suffered throughout our navigation along the coast of Tartary, are constantly breaking, and we only replace the very ends, fearing that we may run out."

Before resorting to the methods of nourishment such as those described in Magellan's log, the heroes of these unexplored sea territories were condemned to a miserable everyday routine. Live cattle and fowl embarked aboard were bulky

Top left:
The *Recherche* and the *Espérance* captained by Joseph-Antoine Bruny d'Entrecasteaux. Watercolor by Frédéric Roux (1805-1874).

Stowing plan and sectional view of a ship. Colbert album, seventeenth century.

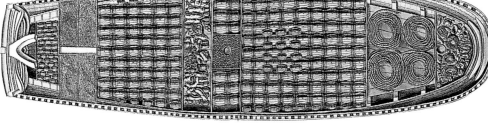

1. coupe des plattes Varangues, 2. coupe des Varangue de fonds entre les façons, 3. carlingue ou contrequille 4. laquille 5. l'estambot 6. gouvernail 7. l'estrauc 8. la hauteur du l'est 9. les courbes de la poulaine 15. gorgere de poulaine 16. les ferches 13. les arpes 14. caisse aux poudres 19. caisse aux gargousses 20. fosse aux cables 21. 18. fouttes aux gargousses vers lusant 24. sep de grand drisse 23. l'escoutille 24. faux ponts 25. foute au pain 26. corridor pour la distribution desdites foutes 27. galleries pour Remener aux coups de canons 28. plancher pour la distribution des victuailles 29. chambre aux poudres voilles 30. fosse aux lions 31. l'escoutille pour la foute aux poudres 32. chambre pour le rechange du gouvernail 33. premier pont 34. fainte barbe 35. barre du gouvernail 36. canons des premiere batteries 38. cabestan double 39. grand mast coupe avec la meche 40. les 8. l'sles foubz le pont l'assemblage des jumelles avec la meche 42. cabestan fimple 43. mast de beaupre 43. la 41. les premieres et secondes bittes 44. mast du grand mast 44. deuxieme pont 45. chambre mizaine coupe de mesme que le grand mast 44. deuxieme pont 45. chambre gatte 46. les amarres dans les escubiers 47. drisse de grand vergue 48. des volontaires 49. offices 50. l'escalliers 51. mast dartimon 53. les parqs pour les moutons 54. cages pour les poulles mast dartimon 53. les parqs pour les moutons 54. cages pour les poulles 55. cuisines 56. fours 57. troisieme pont 58. chambre du conseil 59. chambre des officiers 60. corps de garde 61. balustres pour le mouvement de la manuelle du gouvernail 61. bitte ou s'amarrent les grande bras 63. les canons dehors montes sur leurs affus 63. bitte pour basse dancer 67. grue ou bossoir dancer 65. bitte pour basse de grand voille 69. l'escouets 70. cargues de grand voille 69. l'escouets 70. l'escouets 71. l'escouets de mizaine 73. l'escouets 73. cargues

but offered fresh food. The salted meats were eaten next, although they spoiled rapidly, followed by dried beans and vegetables and hardtack, in which weevils and tropical insects brought on board with the firewood for the kitchen thrived. Louis-Antoine de Saint-Germain, an irascible but fairly justified critic of Bougainville, noted this anecdote in his personal diary: "Yesterday I ate a rat with the prince of Nassau. We found it excellent." Bougainville also recorded this difficult period of their voyage: "The remaining provisions were so rotten and smelled so cadaverous that the hardest moments of our miserable days were when the bell rang, indicating that we were to take this disgusting, unhealthy food." The water smelled excessively rancid, due to the natural chemical reactions caused by the organic materials in the wood of the barrels, which transformed the sulfates contained in the spring water into noxious sulfides.

Many records were kept on board these ships: the logbook, the official report for the mission, personal diaries, of course, and letters, which carried good or bad news to distant destinations. One of the characteristics of the interminable voyages was isolation and solitude. These men—who, in the words of Anacharsis, were "neither died nor alive"— were cut off from any news of their families or the world, limited to a few letters which, by some miracle, may have reached them on the opposite ends of the Earth.

In June of 1793, d'Entrecasteaux, who was looking for Lapérouse in the labyrinth of one of the most unhealthy regions on Earth, around New Guinea and the Solomon Islands, was forced to sail as quickly as he could to Java, due to the illness that was decimating his crew. Jean-Michel Huon de Kermadec, captain of the *Espérance,* was already dead. The admiral then also passed away at sea. The expedition's new leader, Hesmivy d'Auribeau, anchored off Surabaya at dawn on October 19, and sent a skiff to the Dutch governor's residence requesting asylum and help for his sick crew. He knew, since his port of call at the Moluccas, that France was at war with Austria, but he was comforted by the safe conduct received from the Estates General of The Hague, which covered Lapérouse's research mission. In the morning of October 25, a Malaysian *prao* finally brought a message from the liaison officer: "I am a

Letter from second surgeon Gauffre to ship captain Hesmivy d'Auribeau, aboard the *Espérance*, August 12, 1793. The three successive captains of the expedition sent out to find Lapérouse all died during the voyage.

prisoner of war; France is at war with Holland and all the powers of Europe. The Assemblée Nationale was dissolved and replaced by the Convention, which has arrogated itself supreme powers without the investiture of the nation. Our country, half conquered by foreign armies, is on the brink of anarchy, the ravages of a civil war. The king has been beheaded." These castaways exploring the world were suddenly precipitated into a revolution that was taking place without them. Auribeau, the last commander of this community in distress, died suddenly on August 29. There were rumors in Surabaya that he had been poisoned.

In 1825, when Dumont d'Urville returned home from his round the world journey under the orders of Louis Dupperey, he learned that his first son had died two years earlier. He experienced this same trauma once again, on arriving in Valparaiso in 1838, where he found mail from France announcing the death eight months earlier of his youngest son, a victim of cholera. The pathetic letter from Adèle d'Urville is an apt expression of the desperate consequences of long-term travels: "When you receive this letter, you will have finished the work on the ice. You will come back then, won't you? This is my only desire. Glory, honor, wealth, I curse them. I have paid too dearly for them. Come, I beseech of you by the prayer I send, by those of our angels. I no longer pray to God, he has cursed me." And those of his eldest son: "Goodbye, dear father. Maman beseeches and begs you by all the mot sacred sentiments to return as quickly as possible. Why do you have to make this voyage? We would still have the poor child and we would all be together, while your departure has destroyed everything." Of course, Dumont d'Urville continued his mission. It would continue for two and a half years, during which he would discover the Adelie Coast in Antarctica.

Even worse for these explorers of the hidden side of the Earth is that they were traveling into an absolute void, without any other ways of communicating with the Western world than via the American ports and the European East Indies and Asian trading companies. Dumont d'Urville learned from Queen Faka-Kana at Tonga-Tabou that "several years before d'Entrecasteaux arrived, two large ships, similar to ours, with canons and many Europeans, had anchored at Namouka, where they remained ten days. Their flag was all white."

Page from the *Account of Two Voyages in the Southern Seas and the Indies, by M. de Kerguelen* (1782).

Background:
Departure from Saint-Croix, April 23, 1816.

Top left:
The Astrolabe *and the* Zelée
Getting Free of the Ice
Floes, February 9, 1838.
The frigates were blocked
at the edge of the barrier ice
that covered the Weddell
Sea, while the sailors
sought, without success,
to continue southward.
Lithograph from Louis
Le Breton. Atlas of Dumont
d'Urville's second voyage
(1837-1840).

Bottom left:
Running Before the Strong
West Wind off the Cape
of Good Hope, at latitude
44° S.
Painting by Augustus Earle,
1824.

Below:
Commander Jean-Baptiste
Charcot in uniform,
aboard the *Pourquoi Pas?*,
August 23, 1931.
Watercolor and black pencil
drawing by Louis Montagne
(1879-1960).

They were also searching for Lapérouse, according to his orders. "An American captain said that he saw in the hand of natives of an island situated in the gap between New Caledonia and Louisiade, a cross of Saint Louis and medals, which seemed to him to have come from the shipwreck of the famous navigator, whose loss is so keenly regretted. This is probably only a very feeble reason to hope that the victims of this disaster are still alive; yet, Sir, you shall give His Majesty great satisfaction if, after so many years of misery and exile, one of the unfortunate castaways would, through your efforts, be returned to his country."

On February 26, 1828, a skiff from the *Astrolabe* discovered the wreck of Lapérouse's frigate, as reported in an emotional account written by Joseph-Paul Gaimard, surgeon major and naturalist with Dumont d'Urville. "The arrangement of the anchors and their bearing, everything indicates that we have before us the debris of one of Lapérouse's ships. This site alone is sufficient to reward us for the weariness of this voyage. It is a joy that we will never forget. To be able to contemplate at ease, after a series of accidents, the debris of this great and glorious disaster, and to feel to the bottom of one's soul that one is worthy of this honor, is a reward that men do not easily earn, and is yet and fortunately, a difficult reward." The mystery of the Lapérouse expedition had lasted forty years.

"The sea is an this extraordinary thing, an element that is so powerful that it transforms the spirits of the people who live on it, altering their desires, dampening their passions, or making them sharper, more violent." Jean-Baptiste Charcot was speaking on March 17, 1936 to the Yacht-Club of France. After campaigns in the Antarctica between 1903 and 1910, this "polar gentleman," in the words of the polar explorer Sir Ernest Shackleton, had undertaken an annual scientific campaign between Greenland and Scandinavia.

Like Charcot, Prince Albert I of Monaco had, from 1885 to 1920, sent his yachts out on scientific research missions and pursued his passion for the emerging field of oceanography. On September 17, 1936, near Reykjavik, the sea spit out onto a beach of Borgafjördr the bodies of crewmen from the *Pourquoi Pas?*, who had been flung overboard by a violent wind in the night; alongside the sailors was the wheelhouse plaque, bearing the words "Honor and Country," the traditional motto of the French navy. "Honor first," Charcot used to say, "because if you do not have that, you do not have the right to invoke the great name of Country."

Credits and illustrations

Abbreviations:
t: top; b: bottom; l: left; r: right; m: middle.

ANTT, Lisbon: Arquivo Nacional da Torre do Tombo, Lisbon.
BN, Lisbon: Biblioteca Nacional, Lisbon.
BC, Rome: Biblioteca Casanatense, Rome.
BNF, Paris: Bibliothèque Nationale de France, Paris.
MNAA, Lisbon: Museu Nacional de Arte Antiga, Lisbon.
PML, New York: Pierpont Morgan Library, New York.
RMN: Réunion des Musées Nationaux, Paris.
SHAT, Vincennes: Service historique de l'armée de terre, Château de Vincennes.
SHM, Vincennes: Service historique de la Marine, Château de Vincennes.

Cover: Hawaii, Molokai and Mokapu islands. © Fotogram-Stone Images-Richard Cooke.
Inside front and back cover: Mar of Brazil and West Africa. Anonymous Franco-Portuguese atlas, circa 1583. Koninklijke Bibliotheek, The Hague. Museum photograph.
p. 1: © Fotogram-Stone Images, Paris.
pp. 2-3: Title page. Reefed main topsail and foresail. Sketch by Charles-Alexandre Lesueur (1776-1846). Muséum d'Histoire Naturelle, n° 38 001, Le Havre. Photo Art Images.
pp. 4-5: Photo Olivier Grunewald.
p. 6: Dutch ship from the second half of the 16th century. Engraving by Franz Huy, circa 1516, from Pieter Bruegel. Institut Néerlandais, Paris. Frits Lugt collection. Museum photograph.
p. 8-9: The world of fools. Anonymous hand-painted engraving, circa 1590. BNF, Paris. Maps and drawings. BNF photograph.
p. 11: *The Treasures of the Sea*. Jacopo Zucchi (1541-1590). Galerie Borghese, Rome. © Scala.
pp. 12-13: Detail of *Saint Ursula the Martyr and the 11,000 Virgins.* Santa Auta altarpiece, circa 1520, attributed to Cristovào de Figueiredo and Garcia Fernandes. MNAA, Lisbon. Photo Divisào de Documentaçāo Fotographica. Instituto Portugues de Museus, Lisbon, photo José Pessoa.
p. 14: *Oekoumène.* Painting on parchment by Francesco di Antonio del Chierico, in Ptolemy's *Cosmographia* translated into Latin by Jacopo d'Angelo, circa 1465-1470. BNF, Paris. Photo BNF.
p. 15: D. Joào II. 15th-century miniature (after 1485). *Livro dos Copos,* ANTT Lisbon, Cartorio de Santiago. Photo Paulo Cintra and Laura Castro Caldas.
p. 17: Portuguese hemisphere. *Crónica del Rei D. Afonso Henriques,* by Duarte Galvào. First half of 16th century. Biblioteca publica municipal do Porto. Photo Paulo Cintra and Laura Castro Caldas.
p. 19: Aboard the caravel *Boa Esperança.* Photo François Bellec.
p. 20: Detail of *Saint Ursula the Martyr and the 11,000 Virgins.* Santa Auta altarpiece, circa 1520, attributed to Cristovào de Figueiredo and Garcia Fernandes. MNAA, Lisbon. Photo Divisào de Documentaçāo Fotographica. Instituto Portugues de Museus, Lisbon, photo José Pessoa.
p. 21: *Guia Nautico de Evora,* circa 1516. Biblioteca pública e Arquivo Distrital de Evora.
p. 22: Warriors and musicians. Bronze plates (lost-wax process) from Benin. 16th-17th centuries. Musée de l'Homme, Paris. Photo B. Hatala.
p. 23: Portuguese man bearing an arm. Bronze relief (lost-wax process) from Benin. 16th-17th centuries. Museum für Völkerkunde, Berlin. © Werner Forman/AKG, Paris.
p. 24: Nautical hemisphere. First works by Jacques Devaulx, pilot from Le Havre. 1538. BNF, Paris. © Photothèque Hachette.
p. 25: Planisphere by Sebastian Cabot, 1544. (Detail of the Eastern section). BNF, Paris, Maps and drawings. Photo BNF.
pp. 26-27: Photo Olivier Grunewald.
p. 29: Map of the Cape of Good Hope. *Roteiro* by Francisco de Roís, 1513-1516. Assemblée Nationale library, Paris. Photo Assemblée nationale library.
p. 30: D. Vasco da Gama. Woodcut from the manuscript *Lendas da India* by Gaspar Correira. Circa 1550-1563. BN, Lisbon.
p. 31: Illumination of volume four of *Leitura Nova* by King D. Manuel. (detail) Mid 16th century. ANTT, Lisbon. © Loirat/ Explorer.
p. 32: Log of Vasco da Gama's journey, attributed to Alvaro Velho. Copy, mid-16th century. Biblioteca municipal do Porto. Photo Paulo Cintra and Laura Castro Caldas.
p. 33: View of Lisbon in the first half of the 18th century. Azulejo from the Sào Francisco monastery (consistory), Salvador de Bahia, Brazil.
p. 34: Nutmeg tree. *Tratado de los Drogas y Medicinas de las Indias Orientales* by Cristovào da Costa, 1578. BN, Lisbon. Photo Paulo Cintra and Laura Castro Caldas.
p. 35: Mozambique. *Roteiro de Viagem de Lisboa a Goa* by D. Joào de Castro, 1538. Biblioteca pública e Arquivo Distrital de Evora. Photo BPE.
pp. 36-37: Portuguese fleet off the coast of Muscat. *Livro de Lisuarte de Abreu,* circa 1558-1564. PML, New York. © AKG Paris.
p. 38: Rug known as the "Portuguese." Persia, 17th century. Musée des Tissus, Lyon. © Artephot/A.D.P.C.
p. 38: Pepper. *Tratado de los Drogas y Medicinas de las Indias Orientales* by Cristovào da Costa, 1578. BN, Lisbon. Photo Paulo Cintra and Laura Castro Caldas.
p. 39: Bird's-eye view of Calicut. *Lendas da India* (1550-1563) by Gaspar Correira. ANTT, Lisbon. Photo Paulo Cintra and Laura Castro Caldas.
p. 40: Horsemen from the kingdom of Cambay. 16th century. Anonymous manuscript. BC, Rome. *Codex Casanatense.* p. 41: Portuguese man sheltered from the sun by a servant. Anonymous manuscript. BC, Rome. *Codex Casanatense.*
p. 42: Nativity scene with gold coins. Book of hours of D. Manuel, circa 1517-1538, attributed in part to António de Holanda. MNAA, Lisbon. Photo José Pessoa.
pp. 44-45: The king of Cambay. Anonymous manuscript. BC, Rome. *Codex Casanatense.* Photo Dedem Automatica.
p. 46: A Portuguese from Ormuz. Anonymous manuscript. BC, Rome. *Codex Casanatense.*
p. 47: Resident of Korassan. Anonymous manuscript. BC, Rome. *Codex Casanatense.*
pp. 48-49: Diogo Lopes de Sequeira's fleet in 1519. *Livro de Lisuarte de Abreu,* circa 1558-1564. PML, New York. © AKG Paris.
pp. 50-51: Views of Calicut, Ormuz, Cannanore, and Elmina. *Civitates Orbis Terrarum* (1572-1618) Georg Braun, engraved by Frans Hogenberg. Bibliothèque Sainte-Geneviève, Paris. © Namur/Explorer.
pp. 52-53: *Namban-byôbu. Barbarians of the South"* screen (detail). Circa 1590-1640. Attributed to Kano Naizen. MNAA, Lisbon. Photo Francisco Matias.
p. 54: Portrait of D. Afonso de Albuquerque. Anonymous Portuguese painting on wood, mid-16th-century. MNAA, Lisbon. Photo Luis Pavão.
p. 55: *The Castle of Batavia.* Painting by A. Beeckman, 1656. Rijksmuseum, Amsterdam. Photo KIT.
pp.56-57: The New World. Portulan de Juan de la Cosa. 1500. Museu Naval, Madrid. © Artephot/Oronoz.
p. 58: *The Virgin of the Navigators.* Altarpiece by Aléjo Fernandez, 1497, for the *Casa de Contratación.* Alcazar de Séville. © J. P. Nacivet/Explorer.
p. 59: Portrait of Christopher Columbus. Anonymous miniature on parchment from the Spanish school. 16th century. Musée National de la Renaissance, Ecouen. © Giraudon.
p. 61: Ex-voto of Mataro. Catalon votive piece. Mid-15th century. Netherlands Maritiem Museum Prinz Hendrik, Rotterdam. Photo du musée.
pp. 62: Clock attributed to Hans Schlottheim, known as "Charles V treasure ship." 16th century. Detail of the lookout sounding the time. Photo RMN-t. Lewandovski.
p. 63: Automated clock attributed to Hans Schlottheim, known as the "Charles V treasure ship." 16th century. Détail. © Giraudon.
pp. 64-65: Photo Olivier Grunewald.
p. 66: Tapuyan man. Illustration from a bestiary by Zacharias Wagner, circa 1634. Staatliches Kupferstichkabinett. Dresde. © AKG Paris.
p. 68: *The French Arrive in Port Royal.* Hand-colored engraving by Théodore de Bry from Jacques Lemoyne de Morgues. Voyage by Jean Ribault and René de Laudonnière to Florida. 1562-1565. *Grands Voyages* 1591. SHM, Vincennes. Photo SHM.
p. 69: Indians of the Caribbean. *Géographie du Monde* by Artus Fonnant. 1633. SHM, Vincennes. And enlarged detail.
p. 70: *How the Portuguese Sent a Second Vessel to Locate Me.* Handc-colored engraving by Théodore de Bry from a woodcut and story by Hans Staden. *Grands Voyages,* 1592. SHM, Vincennes. Photo SHM.
p. 71: *Flying fish.* Hand-colored engraving by Théodore de Bry from a woodcut and story by Hans Staden. *Grands Voyages,* 1592. SHM, Vincennes. Photo SHM.
p. 73: *Pacoba* and *Zaranga.* Banana and orange. Watercolors by Zacharias Wagner, circa 1634. Staatliches. Kupferstichkabinett. Dresden. © AKG Paris.
p. 74: *Hans Staden's shipwreck.* Hand-colored engraving by Théodore de Bry from a woodcut and story by Hans Staden. *Grands Voyages,* 1592. SHM, Vincennes. Photo SHM.
p. 75: *Mulatto smoking.* Drawing by Charles Plumier. 1688. BNF. © AKG Paris.
p. 76: Gathering the fruit named *Pacona.* Engraving by *Histoire d'un voyage fait en la terre du Brésil* by Jean de Léry, 1578.
p. 77: Printed version of the letter from Columbus to Luis de Santangel concerning his first voyage, written at sea in February-March 1493. Museo de America, Madrid. © Artephot/Oronoz.
pp 78-79: Photo Olivier Grunewald.
p. 80: Huehueteotl, god of fire and mother and father of all the gods. Terracotta 600-800. Veracruz, Mexico. Barbier-Mueller Museum, Geneva. Photo P. -A. Ferrazzini.
p. 81: Zapoteca anthropomorphic funerary urn, 450-650. Oaxaca region, Mexico. Barbier-Mueller Museum, Geneva. Photo P. –A. Ferrazzini.
p. 82 t: Duho. Traditional Hawaian seat. Musée de l'Homme. Photo M. Delaplanche.
p. 82 b: Tapuya woman. Illustration for a bestiary by Zacharias Wagner, circa 1634. Staatliches Kupferstichkabinett. Dresde. © AKG Paris.
p.83: *Oppidum Pomeiooc.* Hand-colored engraving by Théodore de Bry from *Admiranda Narratio,* story of the trip to Virginia by the English, by Richard Greinville in 1585. *Grands Voyages,* 1591. SHM, Vincennes. Photo SHM.
p. 84: Columbus' signature on a manuscript in the Rábida monastery. © Artephot/Oronoz.
p. 85: Pendants made of a gold and copper alloy, Panama. Barbier-Mueller Museum, Geneva. Photo P. -A. Ferrazzini.
p. 86: The New World. Portulan de Juan de la Cosa. 1500. Museu Naval, Madrid. © Artephot/Oronoz.
p. 87: Colombus' signature on a manuscript in the Rábida monastery. © Artephot/Oronoz.
p. 88: Tupinamba family. Engraving from l'*Histoire d'un voyage fait en la terre du Brésil* by Jean de Léry, 1578.
p. 89: Map of South America, 16th century. J. -P. Coureau/Explorer.
pp. 90-91: Photo Olivier Grunewald.
p. 92: "Captain" from Brésil. *Géographie du monde.* Artus Fonnant, 1633. SHM, Vincennes.
p. 93: The Atlantic between Africa and the New World. Anonymous Franco-Portuguese atlas, circa 1583. Koninklijke Bibliotheek, manuscript 129 A24, folio 11/12. The Hague. Museum photo.
p. 94 t: Amerigo Vespucci by Antonio Giovanni Varese. 16th century. Palazzo Farnèse, Caprarola. © Index-Giraudon.
p. 94 b: Brazilian woman. Illustration from a bestiary by Zacharias Wagner, circa 1634. Staatliches Kupferstichkabinett. Dresden. © AKG Paris.
p. 95: Brazilian man. Illustration from a bestiary by Zacharias Wagner, circa 1634. Staatliches Kupferstichkabinett. Dresden. © AKG Paris.
p. 96 t: Portrait of Amerigo Vespucci. Anonymous, undated. Musée National de la Marine, Paris. Photo Patrick Dantec.
p. 96 b: Copy by Laurentius Frisius in 1522, of the mappa mundi *Orbis typus universalis juxta hydrographorum traditionem.* Drawn by Martin Waldseemuller, and printed in Saint Dié in 1507. © AKG Paris.
p. 97: Page from Cardinal Pierre d'Ailly's *Imago Mundi* that belonged to Christopher Columbus. Copy of the 1483 edition. Chapter 8: *De la quantité de Terre habitable.* Biblioteca Colombina, Seville. © AKG, Paris.
pp. 98-99. Natives of Maragnon. Detail of an illustration from the *Géographie du Monde* by Artus Fonnant. 1633. SHM, Vincennes.
p. 98: North American landscape.
p. 99: Sebastian Cabot. Period engraving from a portrait (since disappeared). The Fotomax Index, Century Picture Library, London.
p. 100: Sebastian Cabot's planisphere, 1544. (detail of the Western section). BNF, Paris, Maps and drawings. Photo BNF.
p.101 t: Natives of Maragnon. Illustration from the *Géographie du Monde* by Artus Fonnant, 1633. Taken from an engraving by Pierre Firens (1613) from a drawing by Joachim Duviert, entitled *Natives Brought to France to be Instructed in the Catholic Faith.* SHM, Vincennes.
pp. 102-103: Hand-colored engraving by Théodore de Bry. *Grands voyages* 1591-1598. SHM, Vincennes. Photo SHM.
p. 104: *Africa and America Helping Europe.* Print by

William Blake. (1757-1827) © AKG, Paris.
p.105: Resident of the *Terra Australis Incognita. Géographie du Monde* by Artus Fonnant, 1633. SHM, Vincennes.
p.106: Symbolic portrait of Columbus. *Les vrais Portraits et Vies des Hommes illustres.* André Thévet, 1584. University and public library, Geneva.
p.107: *The select a site for their fort.* Hand-colored engraving by Théodore de Bry from Jacques Lemoyne de Morgues. Voyage by Ribault and Laudonnière to Florida. 1562-1565. *Grands Voyages,* 1591. SHM, Vincennes. Photo SHM.
p. 108 t: *How some of us, who left to explore the bay, found a cross on a rock.* Hand-colored engraving by Théodore de Bry from a woodcut and story by Hans Staden. *Grands Voyages* 1592. SHM, Vincennes. Photo SHM.
pp. 108-109: Caribbean Indians. Detail of an illustration from the *Géographie du Monde* by Artus Fonnant, 1633. SHM, Vincennes.
p. 110: Caribbean Indians. Illustration from the *Géographie du Monde* by Artus Fonnant, 1633. SHM, Vincennes.
p. 111: *On the military discipline of Outina's warriors.* Hand-colored engraving by Théodore de Bry from Jacques Lemoyne de Morgues. Voyage by Ribault and Laudonnière to Florida. 1562-1565. *Grands Voyages,* 1591. SHM, Vincennes. Photo SHM.
p 112: *How gold is found in the rivers flowing down the Apalacty Hills.* Hand-colored engraving by Théodore de Bry from Jacques Lemoyne de Morgues. Voyage by Ribault and Laudonnière to Florida. 1562-1565. *Grands Voyages,* 1591. SHM Vincennes. Photo SHM.
p 113: *Trophies and ritual ceremonies celebrating the defeat of the enemy.* Hand-colored engraving by Théodore de Bry from Jacques Lemoyne de Morgues. Voyage by Ribault and Laudonnière to Florida. 1562-1565. *Grands Voyages,* 1591. SHM Vincennes. Photo SHM.
p.115: *Tempête sur une côte rocheuse.* Pen, ink, and charcoal. Mathieu Bril (1550-1583) Musée du Louvre, Drawing department, Paris.
pp 116-117: Fotogram-Stone Images/Ernst Haas.
p.118: Christopher Columbus' signature at the bottom of a letter dated April 2, 1502, sent to the Genoese Officiers. Archivio Comunale, Genoa. © Explorer Archives.
p. 120: Map of the Cape of Good Hope and the *Terra Australis Incognita. Cosmographie Universelle* by Guillaume le Testu. 1556. Ministère de la Défense SHAT, Vincennes. © Giraudon.
p 121: Red parrot and dodo. Painting by William Hodges, circa 1773. National Library of Australia, Canberra © The Bridgeman Art Library/Artephot.
pp. 122-123: Map of the port of Callao in Peru in the 16th century. Anonymous Spanish chart, late-16th-century. Biblioteca Nacional, Madrid. © Artephot/Oronoz.
p.124: Title page from the manuscript of the *Relation de Voyage de la Mer du Sud pendant les années 1712, 1713, 1714* by Amédée Frézier (1715) Bibliothèque de l'Assemblée Nationale, Paris.
p.125: Ceremonial headdress from Vanuatu. Musée national des Arts africains et océaniens, Paris. Photo RMN-Arnaudet.
p.126: Title page from *Relation d'un voyage dans la mer du Nord (...) fait en 1767 & 1768* by Yves de Kerguelen. (1771) Bibliothèque-Médiathèque de Valenciennes.
p.127: Photo Olivier Grunewald.
p.128: Title page from *Relation de deux voyages Dans les Mers Australes & aux Indes, faits en 1771, 1772, 1773 et 1774 par M. de Kerguelen* (1782). SHM, Vincennes.
p.129 Page from the *Relation*, for January 1 and 2, 1774. SHM, Vincennes.
pp 130-131: Photo Olivier Grunewald.
pp 130-131 (overlay): Map of views of the austral lands and the northern coast of Kerguelen Island. SHM, Vincennes.
p.132: View of the east coast of the Schouten Islands, Van Diemen's Land (Tasmania). Engraving by Fortier, from a drawing by Charles-Alexandre Lesueur (1778-1846), illustrator with Nicolas Baudin's voyage (1800-1804). *Voyage à la découverte des Terres Australes* [...] 1807. Royal Geographic Society, London. The Bridgeman Art Library/Artephot.
p.133: Sea lion in the Strait of Magellan. Journal by Duplessis, engineer and cartographer on Gouin de Beauchesne's voyage aboard the *Maurepas.* SHM, Vincennes.
p.134: Two penguins in the Strait of Magellan. Journal by Duplessis, engineer and cartographer on Gouin de Beauchesne's voyage aboard the *Maurepas.* 1698-170I. SHM, Vincennes.
p.135: Natives in the Strait of Magellan. Journal by Duplessis, engineer and cartographer on Gouin de Beauchesne's voyage aboard the *Maurepas.* 1698-170I. SHM, Vincennes.
pp.136-137: *The* Eendracht *Leaving the Ijssel.* Painting by Aert Anthonisz. 1618. © Rijksmuseum, Amsterdam.
p.138 t: Fort Utrecht on the Javanese coast in the Bali Strait. Painting by Thomas Baines (1822-1875) Royal Geographical Society, London. © Bridgeman/Giraudon.
p.138 b: Animals found on the Galapagos Islands. Journal by Duplessis, engineer and cartographer on Gouin de Beauchesne's voyage aboard the *Maurepas.* 1698-1701. SHM, Vincennes.
p.139: Photo Olivier Grunewald.
pp.140-141: *A Chief on the Sandwich Islands* (detail). Painting by John Webber. 1787. The Bridgeman Art Library/Artephot.
p.142 and p. 143 t: *Roteiro* (chart) by Francisco de Roís, pilot of António de Miranda Azevedo's fleet, who founded a Portuguese settlement on the Moluccas in 1513-1516. Assemblée Nationale library, Paris.
p.143 b: Moluccan women and clove tree. *Géographie du Monde* by Artus Fonnant. 1633. SHM, Vincennes.
p.144 tl: Australian native. Drawing by Nicolas-Martin Petit. *Voyage de découvertes aux terres australes* by Nicolas Baudin 1800-1804. Muséum d'Histoire Naturelle, Le Havre.
p.144 tr: Masked warrior from the Karakakoua Bay on the Sandwich Islands (Hawaii). Engraving by R. Benard from a watercolor by John Webber. 1779. Cook's third voyage. © Artephot/J. P. Dumontier.
p.144 b: Lithograph by Coutant from Pancrace Bessa *Journal de la navigation autour du globe,* Hyacinthe de Bougainville 1824-1826. Musée national de la Marine, Paris. Museum Photo.
p.145: Stern-post ornament from a war boat on the Taninbar Islands. © Barbier-Mueller Museum, Geneva. Photo P.-A. Ferrazini.
p.146: Portrait of Magellan. Anonymous, undated. Musée National de la Marine, Paris. Photo Patrick Dantec.
p.147 t: Map of Tierra del Fuego and the Strait of Magellan. Drawing by Lord Labat, aboard the *Phélypeaux.* Beauchesne's travel log. 1698-170I. SHM, Vincennes.
p.147 b: Symbolic portrait of Magellan. *Les vrais Portraits et Vies des Hommes illustres.* André Thévet, 1584. Photothèque Hachette.
pp.148-149: *Rio da Prata, Estreito do Magalhais.* Spanish map of the Strait of Magellan. 16th century. Palais du duc d'Albe, Madrid. © Artephot/Oronoz.
p.150 t: Boat from Gouane Island off the coast of Peru, and 150 b: Sea lion in the Strait of Magellan. Journal by Duplessis, engineer and cartographer on Gouin de Beauchesne's voyage aboard the *Maurepas.* 1698-170I. SHM, Vincennes.
p.152: Sir Francis Drake. Portrait by Isaac Oliver (1565-1617) Victoria & Albert Museum, London. The Bridgeman Art Library/Artephot.
p.153: Views of ships heading toward the coast and the bay of Nombra de Deos. Page Francis Drake's last log. 1595-1596. BNF, Paris. © Explorer-Archives.
pp.154-155: Samuel Wallis's *Dolphin,* under attack by natives from King George Island (Tahiti), June 1767. Anonymous watercolor by a member of Wallis's crew. National Library of Australia, Canberra. The Bridgeman Art Library/Artephot.
p.155 b: *Louis Antoine de Bougainville.* Portrait by Jean-Pierre Franquel (1774-1860) Musée National du Château de Versailles et de Trianon. Photo RMN/ Gérard Blot.
pp.156-157: Photo Sea and See/Thierry Zysman.
p.158 t: View of New Cytherea (Tahiti), April 1768. Anonymous watercolor from a drawing attributed to A.J. Riouffe or to engineer/cartographer C.H. Routier de Romainville aboard the *Étoile.* Bougainville's voyage. BNF. Photo BNF, Paris.
p.158 b: Map of the island of King George or Otaheite (Tahiti). Engraving from the original map drawn by Cook in 1769. © Mary Evans/Explorer Archives.
p.159 tl: Tahitians offering fruit to Bougainville. April 1768 Anonymous pastel. Rex Nan Kivell coll. National Library of Australia, Canberra.
p.159 tr: Tahitians. 1842. Drawing and watercolor. Maximilien Radiguet's album. SHM, Vincennes.
p.159 b: Danse of the Ancients at Agana on the island of Guam (Mariannes Islands), March 1819. Lithograph from a watercolor by Jacques E.V. Arago, painter and illustrator aboard the *Uranie,* commanded by Louis Claude Desaulses de Freycinet. Musée national de la Marine. Paris. Photo MNM.
p.160 t: *Pirogue traveling at night.* Drawing and watercolor. Maximilien Radiguet's album. SHM, Vincennes.
p.160 b: *Massacre of Langle, Lamanon, and ten other members of the two crews.* December 1787. Drawing by Nicolas Ozanne. Lapérouse's voyage. © AKG, Paris.
p.161: James Cook. Portrait by Nathaniel Dance. 1776. National maritime museum, Greenwich. © Artephot/Nimatallah.
p.162: *HMS Resolution.* Watercolor by Henry Roberts. Mitchell library, State library of New South Wales. Sydney. The Bridgeman Art Library/ Artephot.
p.163: Double canoe in Tahiti. Watercolor by John Webber circa 1777. British Library, London. The Bridgeman Art Library/Artephot.
pp.164-165: Group of Tahitian women in 1842. Drawing and watercolor. Maximilien Radiguet's album. SHM, Vincennes.
p. 166 tl: Melanesian figures; tr: Lotété, king of the Marquesa Islands. Drawing and watercolor. Maximilien Radiguet's album. 1842. SHM, Vincennes.
p.166 b: Ritual offering of a piglet to Cook by natives on the Sandwich Islands (Hawaii). January 1779. Engraving by Samuel Middiman and John Hall (1784) from an ink wash by John Webber. National Library of Australia, Canberra. The Bridgeman Art Library/ Artephot.
p.167: Hand-painted drawing. Maximilien Radiguet's album. SHM, Vincennes.
pp.168-169: *Death of Cook in Kealakekua Bay in Owhyhee (Hawaii),* February 14, 1779. Painting by George Carter (1781) National Library of Australia, Canberra. The Bridgeman Art Library/ Artephot.
p.170 t: A shaman in Tahiti (most likely a *tahua* [priest], or a charismatic chief with religious overtones, *arii* or *arioi*). Drawing and watercolor. Maximilien Radiguet's album. 1842. SHM, Vincennes.
p170 b: Effigy of Ku-Kaili-Moku, Hawaiian war god. Musée de l'Homme, Paris. Photo J. -Ch. Mazur.
p.171: Mahiole, crested helmet. Hawaii. Brought back by Louis-François Le Goarant de Tromelin (1828). Musée de l'Homme, Paris.
p.172: Village of Nama in Vanikoro. Watercolor by Louis-Auguste de Sainson, BNF, Paris/Société de Géographie. Photo BNF.
p.173: Hostile reception by the natives of Opulu (Apia) in Samoa (1838). Lithograph after Louis Le Breton, Musée nationale de la Marine, Paris. Photo MNM.
p.174: Chief of Santa Christina (Tahua Ta, Archipel des Marquises). Engraving after William Hodges, painter and illustrator aboard *HMS Resolution.* © Artephot/J.-P. Dumontier.
p.175 t: Marine officer and group of Tahitian women. Drawing and watercolor. Maximilien Radiguet's album. SHM, Vincennes.
p.175 b: Sculpted jamb-liner. New Caledonia. Musée de l'Homme, Paris, Photo D. Destable.
p.176 t: Watering up at the haven of Carteret (New Ireland). Watercolor by Louis-Auguste de Sainson. BNF, Paris/Société de Géographie. Photo BNF.
p.176 b: Papuan from Bougainville Island. Drawing and watercolor by L. F Lejeune. SHM, Vincennes.
p.177: Native from Nuka Hiva (Nuku Hiva) Marquesa Islands. Lithograph after Louis Le Breton (1838) *Voyage au pôle sud et dans l'Océanis.* Dumont d'Urville (1837-1840). SHM, Vincennes.
p.178 t: Dumont d'Urville landing on the beach at Tucopia. Février 1828. Watercolor by Louis-Auguste de Sainson. (Dumont d'Urville's first voyage in 1826-1829). BNF, Paris/Société de Géographie. Photo BNF.
p.178 m: Catamaran of Balahou (Fiji Islands) Lithograph after Louis Le Breton. Dumont d'Urville's second voyage in 1837-1840. SHM, Vincennes.
p.178 b: Natives from Dorey (New-Guinea) 1824 Drawing and watercolor by L. F Lejeune. SHM, Vincennes.
p.180: Inauguration of the cenotaph erected in Vanikoro by Dumont d'Urville's crew aboard the *Astrolabe* in memory of Lapérouse's expedition. March 1828. Watercolor by Louis-Auguste de Sainson. Rex Nan Nivell coll. National Library of Australia, Canberra. Museum photo.
p.181: Kava ceremony in Tonga-Tabu. (April 1827). Lithograph by Nicolas Noël after a watercolor by Louis-Auguste de Sainson. National Library of Australia, Canberra. The Bridgeman Art Library/Artephot.
pp.180-181: Natives and mother-of-pearl masks on Aroub Island, Strait of Torres. Atlas of Dumont d'Urville's voyage. SHM, Vincennes.
pp182-183: Transplanting breadfruit from Tahiti. Lithograph by Thomas Gossse. 1796. National Library of Australia, Canberra. The Bridgeman Art

EQVI